A Modest Proposal

for the agreement of the people
laying out terms by which governments
can be bound to act ethically and equitably
in the interest of those they represent.

Luath Press is an independently owned and managed book publishing company based in Scotland, and is not aligned to any political party or grouping. *Viewpoints* is an occasional series exploring issues of current and future relevance.

In 2012 and 2013 Angus Reid toured Scotland, leading a discussion, and placing the words of his 'Call for a Constitution' on many public walls, including the STUC and the Scottish Parliament. He found eager listeners and a hunger for change.

This book has grown from that project to embrace the compelling history of the struggle for civil rights in the UK, and contributions from Scotland, the UK and abroad.

It lays down a challenge to people and parliamentarians alike.

A Modest Proposal

for the agreement of the people

ANGUS REID | MARY DAVIS
and many others

Luath Press Limited

EDINBURGH

www.luath.co.uk

for all those that show their support
past, present and future
and especially Mike and Sheila Forbes

First published 2014

ISBN: 978-1-910021-05-7

The paper used in this book is recyclable. It is made from
low chlorine pulps produced in a low energy, low emission manner
from renewable forests.

Printed and bound by
The Charlesworth Group, Wakefield

Typeset in 10.5 point Sabon and 9.5 point Din
by 3btype.com

Contents

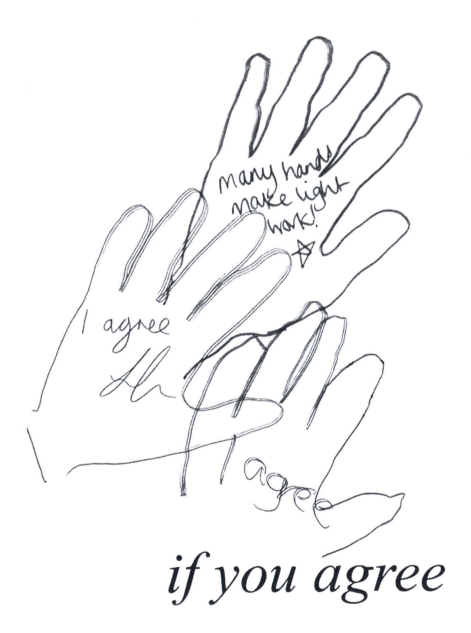

if you agree

Prologue

THE SOMEWHAT LONG title for this book expresses a new way to see and to measure the debate over the future of the UK, starting with Scotland. It seeks to go beyond the constitutional *impasse* and instead it looks back throughout our history, and forward to all those who have engaged with the words of the poem in the languages of the north – many of whom have left incisive comments about the words as they have appeared – as if by magic – in 22 places around Scotland. All this counts as a form of contemporary oral history and is therefore highly relevant to this debate.

So what is the significance of this wordy title and how does it illuminate the book's content? Firstly, the title contains the essence of what we are striving for: an agreement of the people such as was negotiated in the 17th century. Secondly, the title captures the flavour of the pamphlet war in both the 17th and late 18th centuries, a tone that Jonathan Swift borrowed for his own purposes and did so without sharing the optimism, that we have, for a settlement that can embody genuine social change. Thirdly, we have used the words 'modest proposal' because that is how the Levellers[1] termed their own intervention in the constitutional debate; they even used the title *The Moderate* for the broadsheet that articulated their views.

The purpose of this book is to make parliaments concede powers to people and to get on with the necessary democratisation of our society – to empower people and to take a step away from top-down authoritarianism. This characteristic of the present status quo would be just as true

---

[1] The Levellers were a political movement during the English Civil War which called for popular sovereignty, universal suffrage, equality before the law and religious tolerance, all of which was expressed in the manifesto 'Agreement of the People'. They came to prominence at the end of the First English Civil War and were most influential before the start of the Second Civil War. Leveller views and support were found throughout the country and particularly in London and in the New Model Army.

of an independent Scotland as currently foreseen. The future of Scotland and the UK is too big an issue to leave in the hands of parliamentarians: like all progressive change, it is going to take people power to make a just, ethical and equitable settlement. This has rarely been done in our long history, although it was attempted, as we shall see, during the English Revolution. On other occasions, the repressive apparatus of the state was simply too strong to permit any progressive breakthrough of people power and in any case, the people were often not sufficiently united to present a powerful enough alternative to the ruling status quo. This requires class unity, and a corresponding ability to transcend racism and sexism.

To seek 'the Agreement of the People' will once again begin the debate about what we mean by unity, and will, we hope, put flesh on the bones of what has for too long been a mere slogan. *What kind of country do we want to live in? What kind of society is it that we all aspire to?* We cannot achieve unity unless we know not just what we are against, but also what we are for. We call for an ethical and equitable society. We call for the Scottish parliament to debate the words, and then to put them to the people of Scotland. What we want is a commitment, and even though that would only be a first step, we want to make an irreversible step in the right direction that can serve as a leading example to the rest of the UK.

if I as a writer of   poetry
were called upon to give   a form of words
to model the nation's   behaviour
it would be this

ownership obliges
everyone to respect and   to care for
the sacred
to respect and   to care for
freedom of conscience

and to recognise
the gift of   *every individual*
to respect it
care for it   nourish it
to care for and protect *communities*
and
to care for *the land*
and wherever
the land has been abused to   restore it
so that it can support all forms of   life

five principles   five fingers on the hand

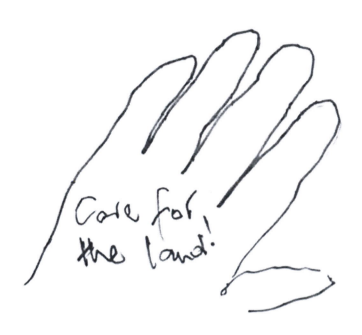

Care for
the land!

Introduction

ANGUS REID AND MARY DAVIS

WHERE IS THE CONTRACT by which we agree to accept the authority of a government?

The absence of a written constitution in the UK leaves the vast majority of people at the mercy of an authoritarian parliamentary class that can threaten our civil rights and liberties according to political whim and by simple majority. The right of redress is remote and expensive. This goes for Scotland as much as it goes for the UK as whole. This unhappy status quo is defended by the idea that it is impossible to define our common values and common identity. This book challenges the laziness of that position. It proposes words to define that consent: words to bind governments, institutions and people into a common social contract. The aim of the words is to put people first, to define dimensions of human existence, and to propose that these values be paramount in any negotiation. We think they are fit for the 21st century: no other constitution in the world, for example, acknowledges our collective responsibility towards the planet.

This idea is aimed at the whole UK, but launched from Scotland because, in the run-up to the Independence Referendum in 2014 in Scotland, the hard carapace of state authority has momentarily softened and there is an opportunity to define a new and better country. The status quo cannot stay as it is, and the political parties are seeking to alter and amplify the powers of government. But where, amid all the political positioning, is there a voice for people?

A constitution must be framed by popular consent. It must originate outside politics, among people. How else could it represent them? A constitution is not an act of government; it is the act of a people constituting a government. The words of the poem are intended as a challenge both to people and to members of parliament by suggesting a form of words that can frame an 'Agreement of the People'. Given such an agreement, the values, rights and responsibilities they embody must then be reflected in the laws, the institutions and the whole behaviour of civic society. This demand is not new: it is the form of the original 'Agreement of the People' laid out by the Peoples' Army and presented to Oliver Cromwell in 1647 in Putney, when the term 'constitution' first entered the lexicon of British political history. And the Leveller contribution to the political tradition of the whole UK should not be underestimated. It was Leveller ideas that gave rise to the only popular uprisings in Scotland, in the South-West in the 1650s, that were lead by neither the nobility nor the clergy. This is the tradition of popular protest that is articulated in the work of Robert Burns.

The words that you can find at the beginning of this book reflect the need for people to have more say than yes or no; for people to define the kind of country they want to live in. They derive from discussions held over a number of years and represent a collective agreement. This book documents their public exposure in Scotland and the public response to them. As I put the words on the doors of Mike Forbes' barn in Aberdeenshire his sister, bringing me a cup of tea on a cold March day, said: '... *if only it were that simple...*' But... why can't it be that simple? A people's agreement is bound to have that virtue: to be simple, memorable and universal. Not to be, as so much political discourse is, partial, secretive and complex.

The way that communities have accepted them across the country raises the question: if communities and individuals can agree to be bound by these values, then why can't their political representatives, and why can't the parliament as a whole? If Mike and Sheila Forbes agree to these words, and their MSP – the First Minister himself – has also signed his agreement, then why can't the parliament act on them?

In each location that they were installed they were accompanied by the invitation to leave a mark of agreement. It was a petition that was made simultaneously across Scotland and inside the Scottish Parliament and it attracted thousands of signatures, including those of Scottish Government ministers and the First Minister. Thereafter came a political manoeuvre by the Constitutional Commission. I was told that the words had been appended as a 'preamble' to a 'draft constitution for an independent Scotland', without my permission, and without telling me what that document was. I was dumbstruck: the words are not there to be added as decoration to a government document; they are there to place ethical values at the beginning of the process. They propose a system of values that a constitution must embody. However, it does indicate that the campaign has met with some success – it is visible – and has forced the government to show its hand as can be seen the recent announcement by the Scottish Government that an 'interim written constitution' will be published in the near future.[1] Naturally, this comes along with the coercive agenda that only a vote for independence will secure these rights. This is where our interests diverge. A constitution is not there to be used by a government as a carrot for a dumb population, but is the demand by that same dumb population to hold the government to account. Hence the need for this book: to show that we operate differently, and openly, and in public. We have nothing to hide. We ask that these words are not merely treated as a decorative addition to a putative constitution, but accepted for what they are: words that have widespread support. We ask that they be debated in a full session of parliament and then put to the people of Scotland at large. This would be a daring initiative. It would show that the government can accept that the 'sovereign people' are capable of expressing a voice, and that they are capable of listening to it and responding. To take this initiative would be to show that Scotland can seize the moment and lead the rest of the UK by example. Were that to happen, then whatever the outcome of the 2014 referendum, it's a victory for democracy.

This book addresses itself, therefore, to the space in between the government and the population at large. That space is everywhere, in libraries, schools, streets, public buildings and private homes, and for the cover of the book it is represented symbolically by the barn at Menie, in the midst of that conflict between capital and community. There, people

---

1   24/03/14 http://news.scotland.gov.uk/News/Enshrining-Scotland-s-values-aa7.aspx

– ordinary people – find themselves with no effective rights as citizens, no faith in the decisions taken by authorities, and with no basis from which to negotiate. This is wrong. That conflict and that space are well known in Scotland, and it is one of many good places that the words have found a home. The cover of the book shows three women at Menie, and the text contains an essay warning women about the history of the past 100 years: 100 years of unfair treatment and discrimination. It's also a reminder of the role of women – often completely hidden – in making significant social change. It is our experience that it is to women that these values appeal in particular, from the grandmother that left a hand-print on the boards in Orkney with the simple statement '... *care for the land*', to Sheila Forbes, the wife of Mike, who stands alongside him and others in resistance to Donald Trump in Aberdeenshire.

As the project has grown it has developed other dimensions, and in particular in terms of that social microcosm, the school community. The invitation to create a School Children's' Charter in two schools, in Edinburgh and Stranraer, has lead to a very significant challenge to the way that schools define their purpose and relationship to children. When the majority finds a voice and uses it to make a simple and direct statement, then it represents – naturally – a major challenge to the prevailing authority. Suddenly a whole community has a dilemma that can best be resolved by applying democracy. And so a whole school votes either for or against a poem, and the very action of voting and extending the suffrage to the whole school community is a great development. However, as you will see throughout this book, the habit of the powerful never to concede rights to the majority is reflected in this social experiment in schools, and the opportunity to democratise responsibility – which is present to us all in this moment – is being squandered. Let's change that around.

This book is in five parts. The first explains the genesis of the words and gives them to you in the other languages of Scotland. Please read them. To see them written in those languages is amazing. The second follows the journey that the words have made around the country in the past 12 months. The aim was to introduce them into the background of many public places, from the Scottish Parliament to the humblest bus stop, from libraries and schools to public cinemas and private homes, and to invite signs of agreement – handprints. The words went up to sit quietly in public spaces and to make people think, and the book is here to give you something to do about it.

The third part, by Professor Mary Davis, the Labour historian, addresses the remarkable history we have in this country in fighting for social rights. In many ways the initial idea of a peoples' democracy was created in Britain. Although it has often been crushed in the moments when that voice has asserted itself, that tradition lives on, and has had a profound affect on many countries and peoples throughout the world. This part aims to show you who your allies are if you fight for rights: from the Levellers, to the working classes, to women, and aims to inform you about the history of those struggles. If they are aimed at school children and teachers because they ought to be on the curriculum and are not, they are also aimed at the labour movement and anyone interested in progressive politics. This is a history of British radicalism, which it is essential to grasp, and to learn from.

The fourth part of this book looks beyond the present moment to a future in which we might all participate in the creation of a constitution. What would be the next step were the parliament to encourage the empowerment of people, and to abide by their voice? These five essays come from different quarters: from the labour lawyer John Hendy QC who presents a socialist view and explores how the rights of the working class need to be safeguarded by a defence of collective bargaining at the workplace and industrial level, and highlights the recent case of Grangemouth; from Alex Bell, who recently resigned as Head of Policy at the SNP and who admires the 'crowd-sourced constitution' as was tried recently in Iceland; from Professor Thorvaldor Gylfason who watched the Icelandic endeavour being destroyed by the factional interests of parliamentarians; from Pauline Bryan of the STUC based Red Paper Collective, that asks what constitutional powers should be for; that asks what constitutional powers should be for and proposes a new federalist model for the UK; and from one of the hosts of the poem in Edinburgh, Danny Zinkus, a member of Unlock Democracy who explores his own hopes for the project and considers how constitutional rights could change our political habits as a community and as a society. If we can take the first step, then many possibilities would open up, and these essays represent the beginning, and not the end of the debate about the kind of future that we can fashion for ourselves.

The last part of the book examines what the recent White Paper has to say about a future constitution and popular sovereignty.

The book also aims to introduce a new and a different tone to political debate, and to wear its independence from any party political agenda on its sleeve. We and the contributors to this book are not dry debaters or paid-up politicians, but artists, writers, polemicists, historians and activists who have reached out into different communities, landscapes, histories and ideas, breaking boundaries of age, race, language and gender, and also breaking down the border of political discourse between Scotland and the rest of the UK. This is a political book full of pictures and full of people: it aims to express itself differently to the run-of-the-mill fare in this corner of the market. Our intention is to allow the many voices, reactions and locations to speak up and to speak for themselves. Ultimately, this book is an invitation to inform yourself, and to agree, and to show it.

This book is a people's contribution to the debate before the Referendum and we are not aligned with either the Yes or the No campaign. We take the view that any people anywhere who are governed without a constitution agreed by the people are governed by power without right. So can this be changed? In our view, the best future for the UK is as a federated state, and we do not support the version of independence that is on offer for Scotland. We see the open debate in Scotland as a rare and perhaps unique opportunity to make a giant step forward for civil rights that will affect the whole UK. As Eliott Bulmer, the thoughtful creator of *A Model Constitution for Scotland*[2] points out, no sincere democrat could possibly support independence in the circumstances under which it is currently proposed. What appears to be on offer in the Scottish Referendum is a wholesale transfer of powers from Westminster to Holyrood

---

2 *A Model Constitution for Scotland*, Luath Press, 2011.

and the creation of a supremely powerful parliament with no people's constitution to constrain it. In which case it would, in Bulmer's words, 'only perpetuate the worst failings of the Westminster system, and ... betray the democratic values which have for decades been central to Scotland's grievance against the UK'.[2] This model of independence would create an excessively centralised parliament with no second chamber whose elite could do anything it wanted and, if history is any guide, that is most unlikely to concede any of its power to people. By being asked to vote 'Yes' we are being asked to participate as spectators in the creation of a new and unconstrainable ruling elite. This is no invitation to create a better democracy, and the choice offered between yes and no does not allow us to define the kind of country we wish to live in any meaningful way.

No. The constitution has to come from outside government if it is to reflect the principle of 'the people's sovereignty'. This is our position, and we take the view that no government has 'power by right', as Tom Paine put it, without a contract with the people. Later on in this book are a number of essays that reflect on what constitutions can do, what the powers are for, and how they can fail. These essays are there to hold the Scottish Government's plans up to scrutiny.

In *A Model Constitution for Scotland* (p. 15) Bulmer outlines the various constitutions that have been part of the SNP's thinking since the 1970s, none of which has sought to discover, to articulate or to represent the values we hold in common, and much less undertaken to be bound by clearly defined values and responsibilities. This is what we can do something about by getting them to debate and endorse this proposal. We hope to change the political landscape, and to change the way a person – any person – can be seen within that landscape. The old hierarchies, classes and ways of doing politics need to be turned upside-down. We call for an agreement of the people. We call for the empowerment of every citizen. We call for a constitution and this is the necessary first step towards it.

A modest proposal.

Are you with us?

The Words

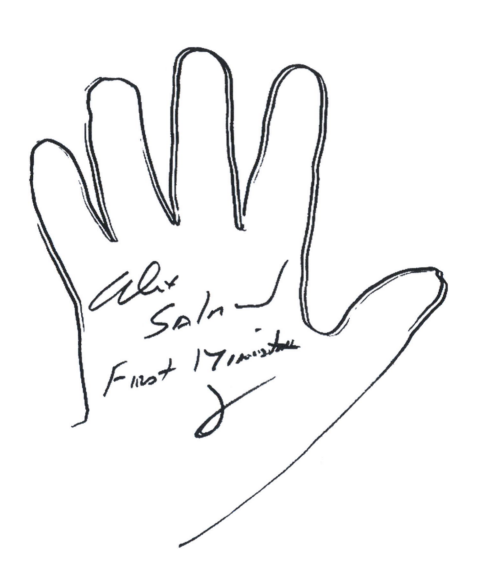

Alex Salmond
First Minister

CHAPTER ONE

The Words

ANGUS REID, *et al.*

IN SCOTLAND WE CAN do something that has never been done before in the history of these islands. To write a social contract fit for our times has been done before but never endorsed peacefully and by majority consent. Were we to achieve this in Scotland we can show the rest of the UK that this is the best way forward.

The most important part of that social contract are the basic principles – what the Germans call Grundgesetz, the ground rules: Grund = basic, and gesetz = law. From these everything else is derived. These would be simple and basic words that define our relationship to one another that a government must abide by. There is no point in having a constitution without 'ground laws' that are known to everyone.

The words in the poem came from discussions in England and Scotland, and these are quotations from an exchange of emails that followed up discussion with a group of ten in Edinburgh:

> ... It is a good idea for a country, as well as any other formally organised society, to have a set of basic laws from which other laws can be derived, and which are considered so important that no new law can contradict them...

> ... I like the idea of 'grundgesetz' – basic givens that underpin every other right, freedom and statement... As with the fundamental laws of physics (which are simple, absolute, universal and stable over time) there will be very few grundgesetz... I believe a Scottish Constitution should enshrine values and aspirations that all people everywhere agree on almost instinctively...

... I agree that law should reflect basic shared values. This can strengthen the authority of a constitution by making clear how specific laws follow from basic principles... an example is the principle from the German constitution 'Eigentum verpflichtet' (ownership obliges). This means that the state expects that owners accept the obligations that come with ownership. This is, for example, how we can justify that they take taxation from us because it defines the purposes to which it will be put...

... I feel that while protecting human rights has done a great deal of good to individuals and states, it has done immeasurable harm to the planet for it ignores the rights of every other living thing. If you believe in rights, then a habitable environment is surely the most fundamental right of all...

... We mentioned the protection of the environment and I think this was a very interesting point: the value of the environment has been recognised only recently and is not therefore part of most existing constitutions: neither those that date from the 18th century, nor the German one that dates from 1947... This is an area in which a Scottish constitution could be at the cutting edge of current social thought...

All these discussions took place seven years ago, and predate the SNP government and the 2014 Referendum. They address themselves to the whole country and to the fact that the status quo is neither acceptable nor stable:

... Without a written constitution there is hardly any protection of rights – any ad hoc parliamentary majority can instantly abolish all previous rights...

... The classical argument ... that Britain already has a constitution that has evolved over centuries... defines a constitution so generally that any piece of written law can be interpreted as part of it, and the term is extended so far that it loses all meaning...

... The British idea of a constitution as a set of different laws with no hierarchy means that laws are in conflict with one another, leaving the field open to all kinds of arbitrary decisions...

> ... Those who want a truly radical and indeed workable solution to the malaise in our liberties should look to a British Bill of Rights embedded in a written constitution, applied by judges who – as in the United States – have the power to ensure that liberties won ... are not abandoned by MPs...

Scotland has the chance to take the lead, but the government has gone about addressing this fundamental change in the wrong way. We should start by defining what kind of country we want to be, and what kind of responsibilities we have towards one another, and then let everything else flow from that. We should start with ground laws that are simple and universally known, and that, as Danny Zinkus says in his essay at the back of this book, that can live in everybody's back pocket.

The poem – or 'the words' as they are known up in Aberdeenshire – propose a way to define those ground laws. To be precisely defined is important, and that is why they are proposed in the form of a poem. It is a kind of armoury that defends the words themselves, as a jeweller might set a precious stone.

I am grateful for some really superb translations into the languages of Scotland. The aim of the poem has always been to make memorable phrases that can live in peoples' minds, and this has been a collective effort, with great results. Just compare 'the gift of every individual' with 'ivery een o wis / ivery een a gift' (Shetlandic) or 'the giftie o ilk ain o us' (Scots); or 'to care for the land' rendered as 'see the grun bide hale' (Scots) and 'ta luik ta midder aert' (Shetlandic). Shetlandic itself has a special vitality and a feeling of practical common sense that reflects an unbroken history of self-government in the islands. 'Principles' becomes 'guides' in Scots and 'steids' in Shetlandic. The word 'steid' means foundation-stone, but also has a political ring: 'steid' was the name of a stone or stones that represented an important starting point for any building project, such as a stack of grain, a home or a communal building which would ensure the basic underpinning was safe against the depredations of time and nature.

Here they are in Scots, translated by Colin Donati:

gin i	as makar
was bidden	to set words
to pit ower the nation's	gaun gate
thae wad be thir	
haein taks aabody bound	
to be considerin o	and canny for
the sained things	
considerin o	and canny for
freedom o conscience	
	and weel ken
the giftie o	*ilk ane o us*
be considerin o it	
look til it	maet it
to haud and to hain *communities*	
and	
see the *grun* bide *hale*	
and whaur	
grun has been ill-usit	mend it
that it fend for aye	aa in life
five guides	five fingrs o the haun

glossary:
gin (hard 'g'), *if*; makar, *poet*; pit ower, express; thir, *these*; gaun gate, *working conduct*; sained, *sacred*; giftie, *unique personal capacity*; ilk ane, *each one*; maet, provide for; hain, *protect*; grun (rhyme with 'sun'), *soil, ground, land*; ill-usit, *abused*; hale, *sound*; guides, *practical controls*

Here they are in Shetlandic, translated by Christine De Luca:

if I as a writer o poetry
wis aksed ta pit tagidder wirds
ta set doon a nation's wyes o wirkin
hit wid be dis

aanin means we man
aa luik tae an tak care o
da sained things
ta luik tae an tak care o
freedom o inmost tocht

an tak tent o
ivery een o wis *ivery een a gift*
ta respeck
ta tak care o ta help had der heart
ta care for, pit a caim roond *communities*
an
ta luik ta *midder aert*
an whaarivver
da laand is bön laid sindry ta restore hit
sae hit can shoard up aathin dat lives

five steids ta bigg apön five fingers apö da hand

glossary:
aanin, *ownership*; sained, *sacred*; caim, *protective embrace*; midder aert,
the land (Lit: '*mother earth*'); bön laid sindry, *made a wasteland*; steids,
foundation stones; bigg, *to build*

Here they are in Gaelic, translated by Rody Gorman:

cumadh

nam b' e 's gun d'rachadh is mi nam ollamh
ri bàrdachd iarraidh orm briathran
a chumadh a shamhlachadh giùlan a' chinnidh
seo mar a bhiodh e:

's ann a tha 'n sealbh a' cur mar fhiachaibh air na h-uile
spèis is cùram a ghabhail don rud
a tha *naomh*
spèis is cùram a ghabhail
do *shaorsa mu chogais*
agus *an t-sochair*
a th' aig a h-uile mac màthar is nighean athar
an aon spèis
is cùram a thoirt dhi 's a beathachadh aithneachadh
coitcheannachd a ghleidheadh is a dhìon
is aire thoirt don talamh
agus àite sam bith far an deach
an talamh a mhilleadh a dhìol
ach an cumadh e gach iomadach gnè den bheatha

còig fàthan
Còig Peathraichean Chinn Tàile 's na Còig Peighinnean

òrdag sgealbag MacIlleathain Fionnlagh Fada
'S Màiri Bheag an Airgid

Here they are in Latin, translated by John Lister:

SI UT CARMINUM SCRIPTORI
MIHI ACCIDAT VERBIS MORES
FORMARE NATIONIS SINT HAEC

DOMINIO OMNES OBLIGANTUR

RES SACROSANCTAS
CURARE VENERARI

LIBERTATEMQUE CONSCIENTIAE

VIRTUTES AGNOSCERE
OMNIUM SINGULORUM
EASQUE VENERARI CURARE NUTRIRE

COMMUNITATES
CURARE PROTEGERE

CURARE TERRAM
ET UBICUMQUE ERIT VIOLATA
RESTITUERE UT OMNES FORMAS POSSIT SUSTINERE

QUINQUE PRINCIPIA
QUINQUE IN UNA MANU DIGITI

Here they are in Slovak, translated by Jana Emburey:

keď ako spisovateľ	poézie
by som bol povolaný	dať do slov
model národného	správania
boli by to tieto slová	
vlastniť dáva zodpovednosť	
každému rešpektovať a	starať sa
o to posvätné	
rešpektovať a	starať sa
o slobodu mysle	
	a uvedomiť si
dar každého	človeka
rešpektovať ho	
starať sa	podporovať ho
starať sa a ochranovať komunity	
a	
starať sa o vlasť	
a kedykoľvek	
zem je nivočená	ochrániť ju
tak aby mohla podporiť všetky formy	života
päť princípov	päť prstov na ruke

We have campaigned to put them into the public eye throughout Scotland as you can see from the map and the illustrations in this book.

It sets out to challenge. It's a challenge to the government, and a challenge to people. Everywhere they were installed people were invited to leave handprints of agreement, and comments. These are also spread throughout this book.

Each location was exciting, taking in schools, galleries, cinemas, bus-stops, high streets, windows, the STUC, the Scottish Parliament *et al.*, but perhaps the most exciting was at Mill of Menie in Aberdeenshire, in Alex Salmond's own constituency. If you can afford the golf or fancy the trespass, there is a magnificent view of the words from the 8th tee of Donald Trump's golf course, on the steadfast and much maligned corrugated iron walls of the barn that belongs to Mike and Sheila Forbes.

One of the great pay-offs of going about putting these words on walls was to get to know Mike and Sheila. Sheila works everyday on the factory floor at a fish processing plant in Aberdeen. This was her first letter to me:

> Thank you very much for supporting us against Donald Trump. The film just lets people see what we have had to put up with. We all think it was a disgrace that the police stepped in every time Donald Trump snapped his fingers; and the way they acted towards the filmmaker – it was a disgrace. Thank you for putting up the poem, and thank you for putting the poem in as many places as you could...

When I went up to make the photograph that is the cover of this book, Sheila was at work. As we waited for her I has the chance to speak to Mike, and to find out things that simply are not known about him. He worked for 15 years as a rigger in the North Sea. He was on the neighbour rig to Piper Alpha the night it blew up and he told me that they had seen it 'burning bonnie' all night. He had nowhere to sleep that night as their accommodation was in the floating platform that was being used to hose it down. Yes, he had worked on Piper Alpha and it was common knowledge that of all the rigs it had the worst standards of safety. Why? Because it was operated by the American-owned Occidental who, as has been documented in a recent film, put production and profit above all other considerations. They had continued to work the rig even when they had to do essential maintenance. They had continued to pump oil and gas from the neighbour rigs through it, even as it blazed. Much of the SNP's case for independence has always rested on the notion that this is Scotland's oil but this is hardly borne out by Mike's experience. Who owns the oil? Who owns the profit? How do the majority of working people benefit from an industry whose profit goes elsewhere, into the pockets of trans-national corporations? The problem is not solved by independence, but by addressing the ownership of national resources and the benefit won't come until this fundamental question is addressed. This problem found an echo in Mike's experience with Donald Trump: the government had, once again, lined itself up behind the interests of speculative and foreign capital to the detriment of both Scottish people, and the land itself. As Mike said memorably in the film: he had voted SNP for his whole life, but never again. He may fly the saltire, but he had become wise to the underlying economic exploitation that was hidden behind the simplifications of the nationalist message.

The film, *You've been trumped*, hadn't given me the picture of these two as working-class people, and also hadn't shown the community in which they live: the large extended family that lives and works at Menie. He told me all this while hammering out body parts for a tractor he was restoring, and painting duck-egg blue. And no, he told me, he hadn't put that anti-Trump graffiti on the walls, but then again, he hadn't taken it off!

It took a lot of work to get the words up on Mike's doors. The wood was weathered from the East wind, and I had to melt each letter into the flaky timber. I told Mike that when I put the same poem in the Scottish Parliament and requested handprints of agreement, as I had done everywhere else, the MSPs had marched past more or less oblivious and I had despaired for the success of the mission. Who pays attention to art? Who stops to read a poem? But I was learning the rhythm by which the Parliament goes about its business, and it all comes to a crescendo on Thursdays, the day of First Minister's Questions. The minutes in which the MSPs left the chamber were the minutes of make-or-break for the project. And suddenly, fate threw me a chance. Alex Salmond, hitherto surrounded by many people, was suddenly marooned, momentarily alone, waiting for a lift. I had been brushed off by so many others that by now I had nothing to lose. So I collared him and I explained the project to him then just as I explain it here.

It's odd to meet someone well known and powerful. It's a bit like meeting Mickey Mouse. You feel that you know them intimately, and yet you've never met them. But Alex Salmond gave me five minutes. We had a slightly bizarre conversation and then he read the poem and, in a gesture that filled me with glee, he took the cheap marker pen that dangled by a string and with the words 'I haven't done this since primary school' he left a decisive and clear handprint of agreement bang in the middle, at the top. A handprint, a signature, and the words 'First Minister'.

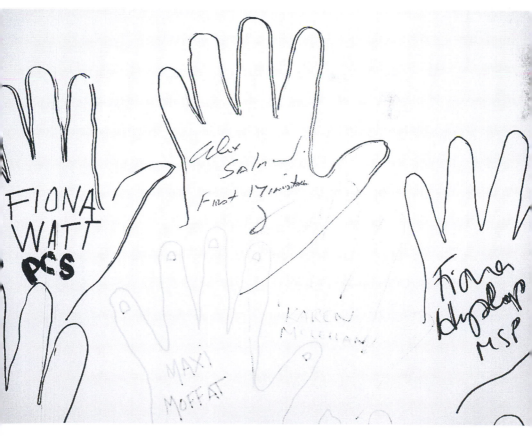

I still feel grateful to him. Kenny MacAskill had sponsored the exhi-
bition in the parliament, but I had felt like a freak-show at the fair up
until Alex Salmond signed it. I felt that I might be thrown out at any
moment. That Alex Salmond signed it changed that, and thereafter people
flocked to the petition. Within just three days it looked like this:

*if you agree with these principles
please leave a handprint*

That is a work of art, beautiful to behold. That is also, all by itself, enough signatures to a petition to raise a debate in the parliament.

These are the names of the MSPs who, like others around the country, when asked if they agreed with the principles left their signatures and a handprint: Alex Salmond, Fiona Hyslop, Ian Gray, Angus MacDonald, Hanzala Malik, Jean Urquhart, Jim Eadie, Neil Findlay, David Stewart, Jamie McGrigor, Fiona McLeod, Claudia Beamish, Bruce Crawford, Roderick Campbell, Aileen Campbell, Liam McArthur, Chic Brodie, Malcolm Chisholm, Dave Thompson, Alison Johnston, John Mason, Anabelle Ewing, Roseanna Cunningham, John Scott, Christine McKelvie, Alasdair Allan, Kezia Dugdale, John Finnie, Rob Gibson, Graeme Pearson, Mike Russell. That represents a range that takes in the whole spectrum of the Scottish Parliament: the SNP, Labour, Conservative, Green, LibDem and Independent. Coupled to all the others around Scotland (it was up simultaneously in 14 other locations), it amounted to a small (in terms of being only several thousands) but significant movement, and a call for the parliamentarians to debate the principles in the poem. It would only take one MSP to raise a debate. So – how come they haven't done it?

More on that later.

The point was that Mike and Sheila also agreed with it and let me install it indelibly on the doors of their beautiful barn. The point was that Alex Salmond agreed with it enough to lead the entire cabinet to sign it. So – given the fact that both constituents and constituency MSP supported these principles, then why was Trump not being forced to accept them? Why was it not being spelled out to him that it was the view of both people *and* government that in this country his ownership of land meant that he had responsibilities towards the communities and the good health of the land itself?

Mike greeted this with a weary, wry smile. I told Mike that I loved his barn because to me these walls were the most political walls in Scotland. There, at the very site of conflict is where you need your principles. Exactly there, on the assembly of worn wood and corrugated iron, where capitalism threatened, and slandered and spat upon the community.

Then Mike told me that after the film had been broadcast, a van-full of guys had come up from 'down south' (wherever that is) with pickaxes, determined to destroy the golf course. They had come in the middle of the night, and Mike had been fortunate to intercept them. He had needed to muster every last atom of authority, and he sent them away. They were very disappointed, he said. But he had given them a lecture. Violence is the weapon of people like Trump, he had said. Here – and his gesture took in the outbuildings at Menie – here, we fight with words.

At that point Sheila arrived back from work, driving Mike's swish reconditioned Jag, we called Mike's mother and sister from their tea, and made the picture.

What a statement.

Words. We fight with words.

* * *

The words make a system. It's easy to explain. None of these values can defend themselves; they can only be defended by consensus. Otherwise they are helpless.

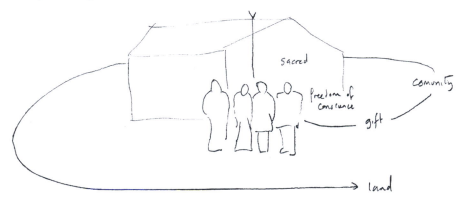

It goes for all of them: the *sacred* cannot defend itself, and nor can *freedom of conscience*. For either to exist requires the respect and care of other people. The words 'freedom of conscience' define the short-lived tradition of tolerance in this country. They were the words coined and used by the New Model Army to defy Cromwell when they refused to invade Ireland and declared that they saw no reason to deprive any freeborn Irishman of his liberty. Cromwell had to purge the Levellers from the New Model Army in order to fight the Scots and the Irish. These words have been abused – clearly! – but they have also survived and they must be at the centre, well known and understood, of a constitution.

They also touch a nerve. The 'Solemn Testimony of Intolerance', a document from the Scottish Presbyterian government of the same revolutionary period in Britain expressly rejects freedom of conscience. This is a Scots voice from the past: the voice of self-righteous theocratic Calvinism. Today, and as we look to the future, I hope we can agree that intolerance is wrong, to call an end to that way of thinking, and to embrace and accept the difference of other people.

In order to imagine *the gift* it is useful to think in terms of a child, or a prisoner, or someone needing help. The gift in such a person must be nourished or it may never be found, and never be given.

As the case of Menie demonstrates, it takes a movement to defend a *community* when that community is held in scorn by the combined forces of the capitalist profiteer, the council, the police and the government. The defence of Menie shows that these values animate people, and are held in common. Andy Murray may have won Wimbledon, but he lost to Mike in the competition for 'Top Scot', gathering more votes than all the sportsmen combined. He told me that he had no idea what to wear for the ceremony. That result was just so encouraging: that a free poll of people in Scotland stands behind the working man.

And, as the case of Menie also shows, *the land* is defenceless to the bulldozers of speculative capital. A concerted effort can halt that kind of destruction, but only temporarily, and it cannot be forgotten that now, after seven years of attrition and with the First Minister directly involved as constituency MSP, the case it still not resolved.[1] How much easier

---

1 There remain, for the record, at least five outstanding issues above and beyond the legality of the whole planning permission and development in the first place: (1) The water has never run properly since Trump cut it off; (2) There is an

would it have been to defend those dunes had it been possible to say: Stop! You cannot destroy the landscape. You cannot slander and undermine a community. That is unconstitutional!

This is why it is important to see the conflict at Menie through the lens of the bigger picture: just what kind of country do we want to live in? One that permits that kind of abuse, or one that stops it?

The resistance at Menie may succeed, or it may fail, but it has shown that there is a consensus that can stand on principle: there is a collective will. It has found images for itself: a hand, folded up to make a fist, and across the knuckles the word S T O P. It makes for a potent combination with the poem: open the hand, count out the values: five. Close the hand, defend the values: fist. If enough people insisted that the government be bound by such values – by a constitution that could not be altered by simple majority – then every individual would be empowered and assured that there is a consensus, and that the force of the collective will can always line up behind the solo fist that says S T O P. Stop – that violates the basic principles we hold in common as a nation. Implicitly that is already happening in Aberdeen, but as things stand the protest could be useless, because the government could continue to pretend that it doesn't need to pay attention to this anomaly in what it sees as its otherwise appropriate economic program.

This is not to say that the current Scottish government is not interested in a constitution. Far from it. It is obsessed by matters constitutional in the manner of a fat man with constipation: it hogs it, hoards it,

---

ongoing plan for a second golf course that would completely encircle the farm and that the Council have not been rejected but that appears to have been abandoned by Donalf Trump (3) Mike still has no access to the beach for his other livelihood, salmon-fishing, after it was illegally blocked by Trump; (4) Trump continues to claim that parts of Mike's land are his, contrary to the plans and title deeds; and (5) There has been no apology for the years of abuse that Mike and Sheila and all the others have had to put up with and which Trump's son, the site manager, reiterated in a recent BBC documentary. It seems to me, as it seems to most people, that it is the business of the constituency MSP to address and resolve all these issues.

can't take its mind off it, but can't explain it and looks to be in permanent discomfort... and this is because it is genuinely constipated by this issue. This is because, if there is to be a constitution that speaks for the people then this initiative cannot come from the government and their chums, but from outside.

So, this modest proposal is a kind of political laxative. It is a form of words that is not written in legalese, it has no small print, it does not conform to other norms and it has not been commissioned by a quango. It comes from another source: the desire to make sure that we all know the words that bind the government's behaviour, and that we keep human values in clear view.

In this way the principles form another system. They represent dimensions of human existence. The sacred: within you and beyond you. Freedom of conscience: the right to live by your own choosing. The gift: to be recognised and nourished so that it can be given to others. The community: the others around you. And the land: that which sustains us all. When I look at Sheila and Mike, and his mother and sister, I see all of those qualities around them. To be human, says this system, is to be able to recognise human values in another person and accept these values as interdependent, and as collective responsibilities.

If these were our ground laws, it would mean that we could always defend the integrity of human life from the things that threaten it – intolerance, irresponsibility, economic hardship, blind profiteering and all the other familiar and contemporary malaises that blight the world. And we wouldn't get into the dire situation that exists right now in Egypt, for example, of not getting around to the constitution until after the election. What a recipe for disaster: to write a partisan, one-sided constitution that is there to defend the interests of a single political grouping within the state.

* * *

Alex Salmond is the First Minister. He read the poem and signed the petition. And then, as far as I was led to believe, the poem was slipped into a secret drawer in Holyrood, along with the draft constitution, whatever that is.

You may be appalled by the implications of this fact, and be wondering whether such a constitution even exists. That would imply that the government intend to impose it on us in the event of independence. It would mean that the whole process is the wrong way around: that the future constitution of the country does not arise from people, but is a ready-made document that, however sincerely expressed, by the very manner of its introduction cannot be other than a defence of the privileges of the elite.

The truth is that such a constitution does exist, although the White Paper has figured the 'process' by which a constitution is adopted in another way. For more on that see the epilogue, and the analysis of the White Paper itself.

At the time, however, I was told that they might use it as a 'preamble' to the secret document, a decorative addition. I didn't feel honoured; I felt patronised and misunderstood. These words are ground laws, not preamble. I put these words around the country and into the Parliament in order for them to be debated, endorsed and voted upon by the population as a whole. I want to believe that our parliament is capable of this. This 'Call for a Constitution' is not a call for any old preconceived constitution, but a call to empower people first, and then set about the process in the faith that the people will get it right. This is a step we should take anyway, whatever the outcome of the Referendum. The first step is to acknowledge that it is a people who constitute a government. It would only take one MSP to introduce this debate.

But, at the time that didn't happen because of the curious attitude of MSPs. While many of them signed the petition, only seven showed up in Committee Room 2 where 100 people from around the country had gathered to discuss the project, as you can see from their contributions to this book. And only one MSP – Jim Eadie – stayed the course and then simply refused our request to bring forward a debate, despite our collective demand and the obvious popularity of the theme. He was, as all the guests attending the discussion could tell you, 'too busy.'

The purpose of this book is to make that debate happen. To empower people and to take a step away from top-down authoritarianism. You can help by signing the online petition. The future of Scotland and the UK is too big an issue to leave in the hands of parliamentarians: like all progressive change, it is going to take people power.

This book is designed to put the past and the present into your hands so that that you can reflect, and act. It includes a brief history of two remarkable moments in British history when people took power, and knew what to do with it. This is our common history and those initiatives in the past helped to make the world a better place. And right now we have the chance to do the same and make a progressive step forwards.

You will see, as you read, that women have been a crucial force in pushing for a better country and a better settlement for all, and that the battle is not won. Please read on and decide for yourself.

What kind of country do you want to live in?

The Journey

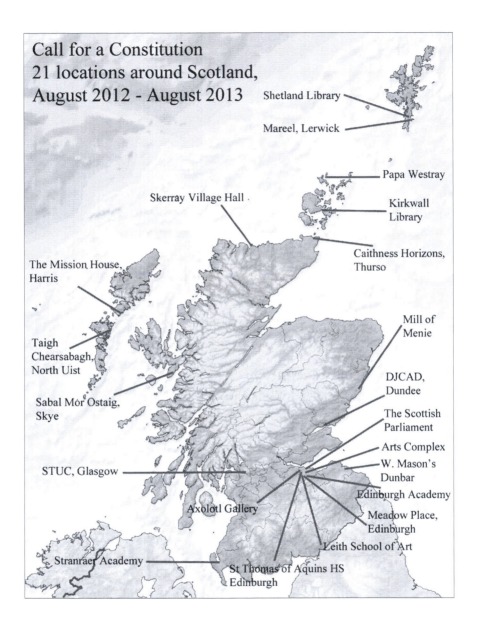

Call for a Constitution
21 locations around Scotland,
August 2012 - August 2013

Shetland Library

Mareel, Lerwick

Papa Westray

Skerray Village Hall

Kirkwall
Library

Caithness Horizons,
Thurso

The Mission House,
Harris

Mill of
Menie

Taigh
Chearsabagh,
North Uist

DJCAD,
Dundee

The Scottish
Parliament

Sabal Mór Ostaig,
Skye

Arts Complex

W. Mason's
Dunbar

STUC, Glasgow

Edinburgh Academy

Axolotl Gallery

Meadow Place,
Edinburgh

Leith School of Art

Stranraer Academy

St Thomas of Aquins HS
Edinburgh

CHAPTER TWO

The Journey

ANGUS REID, *et al.*

WE, IN SCOTLAND, have been called 'constitutionally illiterate' by lawyers and historians because the British state does not have a constitution, but this journey challenges that view. There is barely an area of contemporary life which doesn't have some kind of constitution written by ordinary people, be it a parent council, a voluntary association or a business. It is impossible, for example, to raise any money from a public source without one. The only part of society that regards itself as being above the need is the body with the largest amount of public funds, the government. If there is a part of the country that is 'constitutionally illiterate', it is the government, not the people.

The story of sharing the Call for a Constitution goes like this: it began in Arts Complex, Edinburgh, while Derek Gray was still the artistic director, and it was a response to his curatorial genius. It established the aesthetic of the words on a corner, and a 'response wall'. The showing lasted for only five days but that was enough to draw in the constituency MSP and Justice Minister, Kenny MacAskill, and to ask if he would sponsor the appearance of the poem in the Scottish Parliament. When he agreed, it seemed that, for the poem to be effective it should have a 'social supercharge', and the notion presented itself to show it simultaneously in the parliament and 14 other locations around Scotland, and for each to be a 'live petition'. Why 14 locations? A sonnet has 14 lines, and from 14 sonnets you can make a 15th, using one line of each. The parliament 'supercharge' involved 15 locations, although eventually more were added. This chapter lays out the locations one by one as I visited them, travelling anti-clockwise around Scotland. The images are accompanied by the responses of people from the locations themselves. All this took place in

September 2012; a few installations were temporary, but most were without a fixed end-date, and look forwards, towards 2014 and the Referendum.

Since then the challenge has been to place the poem in places of political importance: in the STUC, in Menie, in Stranraer, and in Meadow Place, Edinburgh. This list is not exhaustive: if you would also like to host the poem, let me know.

In the course of the journey two secondary schools asked me to develop a constitution with senior school children, to address their view of school and education. We did, and the results are compelling. After all, who should make the terms on which education happens: the managers, or those receiving the education itself? Along with the process of writing that charter, therefore, came the challenge to see if the majority would endorse the words democratically in their schools. This would be a progressive and empowering gesture towards a part of the population that will have the right to vote in 2014. However, faced with such a progressive step both schools baulked, and little wonder faced with the fact that in the hierarchy, the parliament itself has not yet proved itself capable of taking such a step. Were the Scottish parliament to debate and endorse these principles it would have a certain impact in the UK, but more importantly it would have an impact across the social spectrum in Scotland. Too many organisations are dictatorships, 'top-down' autocracies, and would function better with the active consent of the majority. One teacher, Matthew Cross puts this very succinctly in his response, and we both continue to hope that Stranraer Academy will adopt the poem. The schools and colleges are gathered together at the end of this section.

Responses

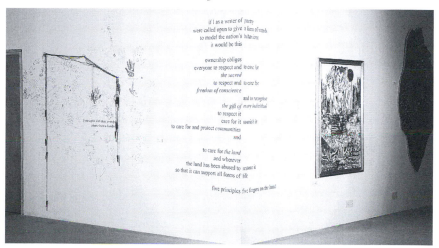

if I as a writer of poetry
were called upon to give a form of words
to model the nation's behaviour
it would be this

ownership obliges
everyone to respect and to care for
the sacred
to respect and to care for
freedom of conscience
and to recognise
the gift of every individual
to respect it
care for it nourish it
to care for and protect *communities*
and

to care for *the land*
and wherever
the land has been abused to restore it
so that it can support all forms of life

five principles *five fingers on the hand*

DEREK GRAY, Artificer, Arts Complex, Edinburgh

The original concept of the avant-garde was to serve the common good, to act as an alternative influence in society aimed at counteracting the influence exerted by the powerful rich. With a few exceptions, the cultural expression of modernist art is that of an atomised society; it is the expression of isolation, of alienation, which takes no interest in the common good.

Today we find ourselves, however tentatively, on the threshold of a similar revolutionary atmosphere to that which saw the birth of the concept of the avant-garde; where long-standing paradigms of an establishment losing grip of its historical relevance are daily being tested in cities around the world; where local-issue protests suddenly and unexpectedly spread like wildfire into broader, political mass demonstrations shaking the ideological pillars propping up an already unstable neo-liberal social (dis)order.

Perhaps the time is ripe to re-appropriate the original concept of the social role of the artist within the avant-garde and to adapt this role to serve a contemporary purpose. I feel with his Call for a Constitution Angus is making a quiet step in this direction.

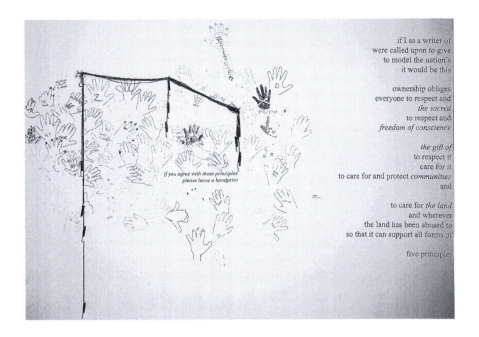

if I as a writer of
were called upon to give
to model the nation's
it would be this

ownership obliges
everyone to respect and
the sacred
to respect and
freedom of conscience

the gift of
to respect it
care for it
to care for and protect *communities*
and

to care for *the land*
and wherever
the land has been abused to
so that it can support all forms of

five principles

*If you agree with these principles
please leave a handprint*

SARAH MASON, William Mason Shoes, High Street, Dunbar

... We like it, and we're going to keep it! If it makes just one person think twice, it has achieved its goal. It's about getting people to stop. And think...! Shoes are my *forte*, not words, but I hope this says enough!

CHRISTINE GUNN, Caithness Horizons, Thurso

Renewable energy is a hot topic of debate in Caithness right now. The Scottish Government's bid to meet promised green energy targets has resulted in serious entrepreneurial activity to exploit the resources of the Pentland Firth and the wind that sweeps our open landscape.

A couple of weeks back there was an article in our local press highlighting concerns from Scotland Against Spin, (an anti-wind farm campaign), that the manager of a local wind farm is trying to abuse the innocence of children by running a 'Name the Turbine' competition. The competition has also scandalised a local anti-wind farm group, ingeniously named

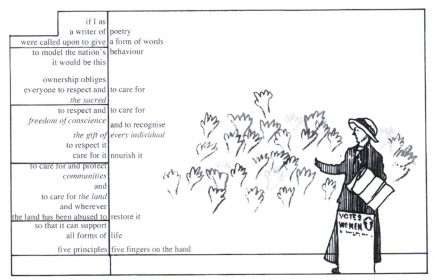

if I as	
a writer of	poetry
were called upon to give	a form of words
to model the nation's	behaviour
it would be this	
ownership obliges	
everyone to respect and	to care for
the sacred	
to respect and	to care for
freedom of conscience	and to recognise
the gift of	*every individual*
to respect it	
care for it	nourish it
to care for and protect	
communities	
and	
to care for *the land*	
and wherever	
the land has been abused to	restore it
so that it can support	
all forms of	life
five principles	five fingers on the hand

CALL FOR A CONSTITUTION AT CAITHNESS HORIZONS THURSO
1:20
ANGUS REID

'Caithness Wind farm Information Forum', whose chairperson told a reporter that young people are being 'brainwashed' at schools, which tell them about green energy 'without hearing the other side'.

The same edition of the *John o' Groat Journal* had a front-page scoop, with the headline:

'DEMAND FOR ANSWERS ON MILITARY POLICE MOVE.'

It appears that MOD police are to patrol Caithness roads to protect us. Against ...? The danger of unspecified terrorists hi-jacking decommissioned nuclear waste from Dounreay? The likelihood that a local farmer might pilfer some enriched uranium mistaking it for animal feed? Who knows? Certainly not Buldoo Residents Association, which represents people living near Dounreay; nor, apparently, the local Civil Nuclear Constabulary [CNC – Yes, we have such a body, expanding as Dounreay is decommissioned]; nor even senior officers at Vulcan [the Vulcan Naval Reactor Test Establishment run on behalf of the MOD by Rolls-Royce for Royal Navy nuclear submarines.]

A member of the Dounreay Stakeholder Group said that if military police were to start patrolling public roads, then the public had a right to know.

'I would express my personal alarm and concern that we have a clandestine police force. We don't know what they're here for, we don't what they're doing and they're not prepared to tell us. I am aware about the issue of security, but there is also a question about honesty and openness.'

The parish pump, you might say.

In my mind, these stories lie at the heart of Angus Reid's 'Call for a Constitution'. To me, the global village appears to shrink and expand at the same time. On one hand, communities, countries and cultures know more about themselves and each other than ever before; one the other hand, it can feel as a citizen that you have absolutely no control over what is done in your name, and there's an uncomfortable sense of being a mote in some corporate eye. What's the point of, and where's the power behind, your democratic right to vote if there is no constitution to state clearly what those who win that vote must aspire to and what principles they must abide by? Why this month in the most recent Scottish by-election (Aberdeen Donside) was there only a 38–39 per cent turnout?

The more important question must be what can we do about it?

Helping promote Angus Reid's project by hosting the poem and response wall in Caithness Horizons where I work in Thurso inspired my only visit so far to the Scottish Parliament building in Edinburgh. Although as a Scot I know that this is where the power of the Scottish people is manifest, it took a work of art to make me travel the 300 miles that mark the distance from where I live and work and pay my taxes to the building where discussion happens every day that will result in changes – great and small – that will impact on my life and those of other Scots.

It seemed important to be present to witness the projection of 'Call for a Constitution' right outside the entrance to the parliament's Debating Chamber, and the hand-marks made by elected members who agree with other people around Scotland who left their hand-marks on response walls from a barn in Papa Westray to a bus shelter in Harris.

I had been disappointed in the response to Angus's poem in our building in Thurso. Its residency was scheduled for only a month and situated where people would not be guaranteed to come across it. Despite invitation, no local school came to visit, and no local politician nor local authority representative left their mark. Most of the people who left a signature as well as a hand-mark were foreign visitors.

Even harder to digest was the disappearance of both poem and responses. I had been present as Angus installed the poem, fixing his carefully chosen coloured letters to its pre-measured wood-panelled wall. I was busy and preoccupied when he arrived after driving up from Edinburgh, and it took a while for my tired brain to register the importance of what he was doing. The next day a small audience gathered to listen to Angus 'launch' the poem. I was moved by the passion with which Angus described how he had been inspired by

Catalan architect Enric Miralles' design for the Scottish Parliament building, and his interpretation of how Miralles incorporated into that design the shapes of the symbolic clenched fist of political solidarity and the open palm of the right hand. In his poem, Angus defined five principles which could be assigned to each of the five digits sprouting from that hand: the sacred, freedom of conscience, the gift of every individual, communities and the land.

After a weekend off, I came back to work and went downstairs to take a photograph of any new additions to our response wall at Caithness Horizons. I was literally dumbstruck to discover the walls were blank: no poem, no responses. No proper explanation of how the work of art came to be wiped without discussion ever emerged. At a staff meeting I had asked whether the poem could remain on its wall indefinitely, given there was no immediate need to take it away.

Whatever the reasons, for me the manner of the poem's removal crystallised its meaning. A community has the right to expect that basic principles must apply to decisions made by those in positions of authority. Without stated principle, any power regime can install or dismantle whichever laws it chooses, and the scope for abuse of that power will remain unchecked. As our global village expands and contracts, shifting territorial boundaries here and morphing cultural identities there, we don't like to think about the fact that we're reliant on an assumption that Western models of democratic representation will always produce benign political management.

The one extended local response to 'Call for a Constitution' came from Jana Emburey, an artist who has recently come to live and work in Caithness because her husband's job demands it. She is Slovakian, and her translation of the poem into her own language was accompanied by observations on how the material comfort of most people in this country seems to blind them to the fact that they are vulnerable:

> Questions do arise when things that made our lives safe and comfortable disappear. British/Scottish constitution is not written for us or for the parliament to follow, the laws we have can be amended by and to suit the ideology of our voted parliament.

Jana hopes that the urge for 'revolution' she senses behind 'Call for a Constitution' is a 'velvet one, like the one I experienced 23 years ago in my homeland'.

The problem that seems to dog the inclination for revolution in the 21st century global village seems to be the difficulty of defining terms: how can the revolutionary state his/her terms when the 'opposition' is just a shade of grey different? How can the inertia of materially comfortable peoples be prodded into mobilisation on behalf of those less well off? What does it take to inspire people to demand that values must precede economic planning, and principles like those asserted by Angus Reid in 'Call for a Constitution' can be written down to form an agreement by the people of our nation, and used to build a healthy community?

We all want easy answers. As the Middle East Spring shows only too well, they're not easy to come by. Certainly, the group that assembled with Angus Reid in a committee room of the Scottish Parliament on 25 September 2013 did not come up with any. But as Scotland approaches the 2014 Referendum, our country has an opportunity – whatever the outcome – to refresh its identity, and to undergo a political health-check. Shouldn't a written constitution be part of that?

The words and the wall wiped clean, and replaced with the brochure 'Scotland – the app'.

PAPA WESTRAY, Orkney

if as a writer of poetry
were called upon to give a form of words
to model the nation's behaviour
it would be this

ownership obliges
everyone to respect and to care for
the sacred
to respect and to care for
freedom of conscience

and to recognise
the gift of *every individual*
to respect it
care for it nourish it
to care for and protect *communities*
and
to care for *the land*
and wherever
the land has been abused to
so that it can support all forms of restore it
life

five principles five fingers on the hand

*if you agree with these principles
please leave a handprint*

Handprint with the Orkney Cross.

GARY AMOS, Orkney Library, Kirkwall

if you agree with these principles
please leave a handprint

Folk in Orkney are often not prone to outward public displays of opinion. So when the installation first appeared in the foyer of the Library & Archive and remained blank for a while I was not surprised. Gradually however, once the first handprint had materialised – more followed. Looking back over the installation now the public contribution seems largely a tide of youth. Young sounding names, smallish handprints, bright colours and a single comment 'Let this be the philosophy for a new generation'. There are other comments less profound, some plain silly but still representing something if not agreement. Other generations are represented too. 'Care for the land' and 'Restore the land' echo the community's strong ties to its environment. Most commonly and perhaps above all, a single word stands out, simply 'Agree'.

KAREN FRASER, Shetland Library

I was not greatly enthusiastic about being hijacked by a campaigning poet on a Friday afternoon. Therefore I'm not entirely sure how, by 5pm that day, I had not only agreed to let Angus Reid install the poem high in the arches of the Library, but to open up on Sunday to let him do it. The Library was not a venue Angus had planned for his poem, but an extra one he thought about at short notice once in Shetland. Once he saw the white-painted arches of the old church where we are housed, and identified a spot for the poem, Angus's persuasiveness and energy took over. Both we at the Library and his cheerfully willing conscripts from Shetland Arts were swept along to make it happen. After all, it's not every day that one is invited to be part of a nation-wide campaign for a new social contract.

The poem is in a difficult place to reach, a difficult place to measure, and the poem ultimately only just fits, inch-perfectly. It is as if it was meant to go there. It might be best to draw a veil over the precarious process by which it got there, which shredded my nerves – but the artist seem protected by an aura of self-belief. Staff coming in on Monday morning were surprised and delighted at what had materialised over the weekend. Customers admired it and added thoughts and handprints to a comments board, and people still notice the poem and ask about it.

Poetry in the Library doesn't just stay in books. We have poetry readings, open-mic nights, workshops and events. Our 'Bards in the Bog' project puts original poetry on toilet doors all over the islands. We like to catch people unawares with poetry. Therefore it's entirely appropriate to have this poem, at this moment in our history, beautifully displayed high on the Library walls, for all to read. Many of the installations have been temporary ones, but this poem fits, and looks beautiful, and we intend to keep it for a long while.

if I as a writer of poetry
were called upon to give a form of words
to model the nation's behaviour
it would be this

ownership obliges
everyone to respect and to care for
the sacred
to respect and to care for
freedom of conscience

and to recognise
the gift of every individual
to respect it
care for it nourish it
to care for and protect *communities*
and
to care for *the land*
and wherever
the land has been abused to restore it
so that it can support all forms of life

five principl...

DONALD ANDERSON, Mareel, Lerwick, Shetland

Mareel is a cinema, music and education venue sited on the waterfront of Lerwick, Shetland's current capital. It has been the focus of lively, and at times bitter debate. The most vociferous claim has been that the money spent on the building was wasted. Since the building opened for business, the attendances have far exceeded the figures projected in the much scorned business plan.

Some months before we opened the venue to the public, and while it was still unclear when the opening would be, Angus Reid got in touch with me about a project he was developing, which involved the installation of his poem, 'Call for a Constitution' in the Scottish Parliament building at Holyrood. His plan was to install the poem throughout the country, in village halls, galleries, and schools – the heart-places of communities. He was enthusiastic and persistent. There was something about the work, something about the way it looked and something about the act of

if I as a writer o
wis aksed ta pit tagidder
ta set doon a nation's
hit wid be dis

aanin means we man
aa luik tae
da sained things
ta luik tae
freedom o inmost tocht

ivery een o wis
ta respeck
ta tak care o
ta care for
pit a caim roond *communities*
an
to luik ta *midder aert*
an whaarivver
da land is bön laid sindry ta
sac hit can shoard up aathin dat

five steids ta bigg apön

installing a poem in the Scottish Parliament. Something about the conviction of the artist. I took it to my arts development colleagues, read the poem to them, and showed them what it would look like on a wall. We wondered together if there might be some way of housing it in Mareel...

Things happened – Angus got funding from Creative Scotland, and his first act was to commission Christine De Luca to translate the poem into Shetland dialect. Shetland Arts' Director, Gwilym Gibbons, agreed in principle to the poem being installed in the building. Angus was fascinated by the large scale of the building, the architecture and the way the different planes interact. He made a scale model of the interior to explore a massive plan: to install the dialect version at huge and prominent scale at the heart of the upper foyer, and to juxtapose it diagonally with a smaller English version on an opposite corner. The majority of the words are lit up and shine in the east light entering through the glass façade of the foyer.

The poem turns a corner down an interior hall, and this, the wall on which the 'thin' side of the poem was installed was also chosen as a 'response' wall. Angus arrived off the boat on the morning of 31 August, the Friday of the first weekend of Wordplay 2012, Shetland's 11th annual book festival. As it turned out, this was a matter of hours before Mareel opened for the first time, and the perfect moment to add this final touch. With the help of Keith Morrison and Jono Sandilands, Angus installed both poems and then went to the pub.

Immediately, the responses were more than enthusiastic. People left their hand-marks on the response wall and this aspect of the project grew and grew. It seemed that everybody had to make their mark. Some people complained about the mess. Within a day the pens were taken down but people just came along with their own pens. Not everybody limited themselves to hands: other parts of the human anatomy began to appear.

Finally, we drew a line. Part of the idea had been to allow people at large to take possession of the building, and to know that it was theirs. The wall allowed that, and it showed people whom they are as a community. It was an experiment in controlled anarchism and, after several months, it had run its course. So, the wall was painted over and a few words from the giant poem were taken down. However, it was now too late to go back. It would be an authoritarian step to return to the original blank walls: this work had helped Mareel settle into the hands of the Shetland community. It is important that people took possession of the walls of Mareel, and even while their marks have now gone, the pithy common sense of Christine de Luca's translation is, among other things, a kind of sentinel to guard that memory.

if you agree with these principles
please leave a handprint

IAIN HUNTER, Skerray Village Hall, Sutherland

In the gathering dusk of a September evening, like a magician performing with wondrous sleight of hand, Angus carried the small but attentive audience at the Harvest Festival through the construction of a two dimensional poem, to convey an eloquent plea for a more inclusive and caring society and how that may be promoted by the adoption of a suitable set of words – a written constitution.

Earlier that day, the installation had been launched at Skerray village hall, the cultural centre of this small community on the north coast of Scotland, the 'back coast'. As an occasional visitor to Skerray, I had not been aware of the potential of this event and had given priority to other activities that day. However, I was arrested by Angus' presentation as he explained his vision and the project to place the poem in a number of locations around the country.

For a semi-literate engineer, it's awe inspiring to see a word-artist in full flight, on a trajectory that's been assembled, mapped and rehearsed before other audiences and other places, especially when it comes as a total surprise. So, suspend reality, go with the flow and enjoy the performance. In my humdrum existence, I seldom get to witness such happenings and was glad of the opportunity.

Later, over a pint and playing the pedant to his Leveller, I brought the conversation back to the reality of Scotland's current position – a constitutional monarchy (without a written constitution!) in an increasingly unhappy marriage with a neighbour who thinks they have primacy over all aspects of shared agreements and estate, including constitutional matters. While other activists were firing up to prepare a campaign to persuade the nation to end this marriage and release Scotland to be all that it could and should be, was Angus' eloquent plea not just a diversion?

Just a few days before these events, I had been in conversation with my local MSP in a west central Scotland constituency, bemoaning the fact that, given the enormity of the Referendum question about to be put to the nation, the level of apathy even among political party members was

s is cùram a ghabhail

haorsa mu chogais

s an t-sochair

' aig a h-uile mac màthar is nighean athar

on spèis

ram a thoirt dhi 's a beathachadh aithneachadh

cheannachd a ghleidheadh is a dhion

re thoirt don *talamh*

àite sam bith far an deach

lamh a mhilleadh a dhìol

an cumadh e gach ion gnè den bheatha

fàthan

Peathraichean eighinne

g sgealbag Ma

àiri Bheag an A

staggering, with only the usual handful of weel kent faces turning out to discuss campaign activities, let alone hitting the streets.

By comparison this sparsely populated small community of Skerray seems always to demonstrate a level of engagement that might be envied elsewhere. Perhaps living close to the edge means that less can be taken for granted, reassurance must always be sought, and perhaps it is the remoteness itself that drives or even attracts a natural selection.

The poem adorns the wall of Skerray hall, both in English and Gaelic. It is not a temporary thing or simply a reminder of an evening past, but a recording of conversations taken place, ideas shared. These conversations preceded the poem, and came with it, and continue: it has been intoned by a visiting rap band, it has added solemnity to a local funeral, it has caught the bleary eye at a weel lubricated ceilidh; these words, it seems, were never and never will be out of place.

The event in Skerray and the later meeting at Holyrood, while stimulating and eliciting interesting contributions from a wide variety of folks, for me served to underscore the reality that the yawning gap in Scotland's societal infrastructure – that Angus has pointed to and that his 'constitution' aims to address – is indeed recognisable by specialist thinkers and scribes who are all itching to address the blank sheet of paper potentially afforded by new sovereign nation status.

Launching the Call for a Constitution in the belief that a groundswell could be developed to the extent that the Scottish and then UK Governments would be compelled to take ownership would seem to be a forlorn hope, especially as those Holyrood folks are engaged in pretty serious re-engineering already. But hopefully, this need, now highlighted, may even be addressed in one of their many white papers.

As I travelled home from the capital, I was buoyed up by the realisation that forlorn hope or no, what I'd witnessed was a little bit of renaissance Scotland, my Scotland, the Scotland I'd prefer to live in: where the artists and makars are free and eloquent to make their voice heard when they have something to say; and it felt good.

MARRI MORRISON, Taigh Chearsabagh, North Uist

'O honey-bees,
Come build in the empty house of state'

Yeats' invitation rang in my ears, when Angus Reid's visit to the Isle of
North Uist, an island in the Outer Hebridean archipelago, was
advertised. He was coming, as part of a tour round Scotland, with a poem
which he was to present to the Scottish Parliament. Incongruous, bold,
delightful! Just what a hectic Parliament needed, I felt, to force it to step
back and reflect honestly on the inner purposes of its spin and rhetoric.

I was reminded too, of the political relevance of the classical Gaelic
bards and seanchaidhs (storytellers) within the societies of the
Gàidhealtachd. Even until the early 20th century the local bard was
regarded as the critical mediator of opinion, presenting the intelligent
line on the issues and people of the day, as well as recording and
reflecting the concerns of the community. The North Uist bard, Domhnall
Ruadh Choruna, and bard, Eachann MacFhionnlaigh, of Berneray
commented poignantly on their experiences in the First World War and
of life, holding their place today as important touchstones for our
islands. Their songs are still sung regularly, and their collections of
poems republished, testament to the tradition of bàrdachd and its
importance as living memory.

Our first sight of Angus Reid was his lean figure clambering over tables
in the café to fix his sonnet in giant letraset on two sides of a corner of
white wall in Taigh Chearsabhagh, the Museum and Arts Centre in
Lochmaddy, North Uist. Displaying the poem so prominently in large
type on the wall was an innovative way of reaching out to our vibrant,
if small and far from the centre, island community. That the two 'sides' of
the poem could be read almost separately was intriguing: the right 'side'
of the print was an almost abstract synopsis of the left, a puzzle to
decode. And Angus Reid was dedicated to alerting other communities –
who might be deemed peripheral – to his poetic message, because,
living far from the alleged 'centre' demands much extra effort in cost and
journey-time.

Space was left beside the poem for comments to be written inside our handprints on a further section of wall as a form of visual legacy and dialogue, an inclusive process, with many of those at his talk and, subsequently, visitors to the café, adding their ideas and reflecting some ambivalence and caution in the march towards Scottish Independence. I was particularly struck by the fact that Angus had painted the poem on the side of the barn of the farmer in Aberdeenshire who had defied Donald Trump's desecration of the environment with a golf course and refused to sell-out to him. Donald Trump's placing of multiple golf courses around the perimeter of his farm seems a vicious and petty capitalistic taunt. I hope the entrepreneur can read and understand the poem.

Those of us who assembled for the reading and talk were in for an electrifying evening. Angus Reid took us through the eclectic and provocative thesis of his poem, that, as Scottish citizens, before we were in a position to vote on national independence, we surely needed to know what it was we were opting into, what national 'ownership' of the land really meant, and which core values we felt needed to be agreed upon, democratically. He posited 'five principles', analogous to the 'five fingers on the hand', (an appealing metaphor), for us to debate, assuring us his take on independence was a-political and that he had no particular allegiance to any political party. Cutting through much of the cant of the day, he took us back to a more ethical form of direct questioning of political/philosophical values, emphasising the 'sacred' nature of all our responsibilities as carers for, and respecters and nourishers of 'freedom of conscience', guardians and protectors of communities and 'restorers' of the land. Five, abstract principles, but together, a potent litmus test for any parliamentary enterprise or piece of legislation. The central question he posed was 'What kind of country do you wish to live in?', a direct message to our MSPs about the forthcoming Referendum on national independence, and a nudge for them to think profoundly about what should perhaps be their major consideration, that of offering us a thoughtful constitution to guide our responses.

He then guided us through a very interesting discussion on the meanings and metaphors the Catalan architect, Enrico Miralles, had incorporated

into the design of the new Scottish Parliamentary buildings. Angus Reid had had unique access, granted by his widow, to Miralles' papers, research and plans, in Catalonia, for the Parliament building. Miralles' inspirational design with the openness of its repeated hand design, and boat and coastline imagery, together with the inventiveness of the placing of the windows and streaming of light was bold, inclusive and revolutionary. Again, the five fingers of its hand reached out to embrace the ordinary people. We immediately wanted to go and experience it for ourselves!

Angus also mentioned the work of Barbara Hepworth. So I digress. Through a university friend, I knew her briefly, when I was a student, and had the good fortune to visit her studio in St Ives on several occasions. I remembered her delight when Dag Hammarskjold commissioned her to sculpt a work for the new United Nations building, and her passionate belief that this might mean a more collaborative and internationally agreed way of overcoming future dissention and wars. She was active politically and I remember her fixing me with a frighteningly penetrating gaze and asking me what my politics were.

'Do you protest?' she asked. 'You must always stand up for what you believe, even if it means being unpopular and fighting for justice.' This has remained with me, and, yes I do.

And now, how to do justice to the sonnet? Angus Reid's dazzling and original poem is an exciting rejigging of the sonnet form, opening out poetic and political possibility to post-modern bards and listeners. His inventiveness here, after more than four centuries of accepted forms, (Petrarchan, Shakespearian et al.), unnerved and delighted me. Getting up early the following morning, I wanted to try it out for myself through my rough request to be put on the guest list for the parliamentary event. The syllables in the sonnet I tried to write were not counted as meticulously as Angus Reid does, but my imagination had been fired to reflect swiftly on my own misgivings about the less palatable connotations of nationalism. Notions of ethnic supremacy, territorial possessiveness, exclusivity, and religious and cultural intolerance, regretfully, appear to lead to worrying and ignorant movements such as the National Front and the EDL. (As a feminist, though, I will always privilege racial discrimination above my 'Western' feminism, feeling as I do, that any racial intolerance is the worst and most insidious form of discrimination on the earth, and directly arisen as the result of our regrettable colonial histories). So I wanted to include in my attempt references to poets who had thought deeply, in an international way, about the plight of poverty and inequality. I had to mention George Mackay Browne's poem 'To the Tibetan Refugees' and Pablo Neruda's poem, 'The People'; my notion of nationalism, such as it is, is a plea for pluralism, loose federations and as many non-imperialistic 'unions' as possible.

Writing between 1791 and 1792, in his *Rights of Man*, Thomas Paine declared what for me was a helpful definition:

> That men mean distinct and separate things when they speak of constitutions and of governments is evident; or, why are these terms distinctly and separately used? A constitution is not the act of a government, but of a people constituting a government; and a government without a constitution is power without right.

'Power without right' challenges the basis of what is meant by democratic representation. Unless the Scottish electors know in advance the what, where and how of the ways in which their rights will be enshrined constitutionally, what will it be that we will be giving our consent to?

So two of us, both cailleach pensioners, determined to be part of what we imagined was to be an exciting and seminal meeting between poet, poem and parliament, travelled from Uist to Edinburgh on 25 September in high anticipation. It was to be our first visit to the Parliament building, a visit both of us felt had been heightened by the insight into the architectural and philosophical ideals Angus' detailed research into Miralles' papers and drawings had given us, during his talk. Not even this, however, could have prepared us for the stunning effects of standing in the soaring, elegiac, floating wood and light of the building. Entranced and altered by the ethos of the place, we explored the public spaces, staircases and openness of the galleries.

But beyond this, such disappointment lay. So, now my rant.

To begin with, the ushers seemed uncertain about the event. Scepticism, rather than welcome greeted us, not a helpful omen. Eventually, things were clarified, and about a hundred of us were shepherded, almost it seemed as an afterthought, into an imposing room with a huge circular table. But, then, there were older school students present, always a heartening element for the tenor of debate. We waited eagerly for the MSPs, wondering where they would sit, since we the visitors had almost packed the committee room. And we waited. Would the First Minister put in an appearance? We certainly expected Nicola Sturgeon, since the Referendum lies in her lap. And we waited. Would our own MSPs acknowledge us? We had half expected them to greet us at the door! Yes, the valiant Kenny MacAskill was present, introduced the evening and departed. Only one MSP, Jim Eadie, stayed throughout and it seemed for him to be a chore.

So I felt deeply ashamed for the scant recognition the event was given by our elected representatives, particularly after the Herculean labours of Angus Reid to raise the issue of constitutional rights around Scotland's periphery. Possibly seven or eight MSPs scuttled in late, and maybe all had scuttled out within about 20 minutes. The parcel of scuttlers included our own MSP. We were shocked that none of them made any attempt to identify whether any of their constituents were present and that, on entry, no one even took our details to alert our MSPs to our presence. So how do we get them to pay attention to our concerns, to place the imperatives of Angus Reid's sonnet at the heart of their thinking?

In the end, we spoke amongst ourselves for two hours, a lively and wide-ranging debate about where to go next with the poem and its relevance to a potential constitution. The school students and their enlightened head teacher and staff had developed Angus Reid's poem into two impressive bills of rights for all school students and staff, potentially an exciting model for development. We discovered a group was meeting to discuss issues of constitution, but that the group was advisory rather than executive. How would the wide-ranging issues we discussed so passionately be heard and acknowledged? We were disillusioned that MSPs did not seem to be bothered to listen to the vox populi, felt sad for Angus Reid and somewhat slighted ourselves. Perhaps we should establish a protest rota and send a poem a day to Parliament?

Maybe nations and their parliaments would be wiser, if they had at their hearts a Reid, a Tagore, or a Neruda, acting as a rebarbative bard of the week or the month, reflecting intuitively and honestly on political debate through the compressed and hard-hitting fist of the poem. There is undoubtedly room in the magnificent foyer of the parliament building for a large digital touch screen to display such poems. After all, the outer walls carry their inscribed quotations in Gaelic and Scots at eye height, making our walking past the building a thoughtful process. In 'Cultures and Habitat', written in 1998, the celebrated ethnobotanist Gary Paul Nabhan states,

By replenishing the land with our stories, we let the wild voices around us guide the restoration we do. The stories will outlast us.

It is my profound wish that wild bardic voices be heard, next time.

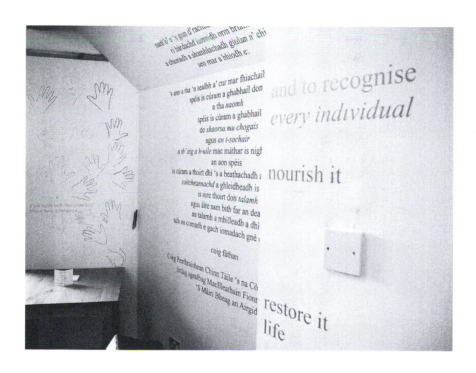

DAVE MOXHAM, STUC Deputy General Secretary

The STUC has no formal position on whether or not the UK should have a written constitution, but we see ourselves as having an important role in providing a platform for our members and their families to have their voice. The poem sits in the central hall of our building, rather magnificent, but quietly in the background. As it was being installed it attracted interest from many of the groups that have offices here, or meet here to hold discussions and events.

The virtue, as I see it, in the idea of a statement of common values is that it is a way to cut through barriers of class, race and gender that frequently isolate different parts of our society. Such grounds laws apply equally to everyone, and create a common ground. In many countries with constitutions it is understood that trade unions have an important and protected role within society through freedom of association and through having a direct role in the way the companies which employ them do business. Why should we aspire to any less here? Why shouldn't the crofter expect to be represented on the planning committee, and the parent on the school board? We need a common ground and the poem is a brave attempt to suggest how we can start to create that in simple and universal language.

NIKOLAI GLOBE, Harris

In the North Room, the outscape is eroded, laid bare. A compass points to a bus shelter, bleak and displaced from urbania, etched with graffitism, another language from a different space, positioned precariously in the exposed landscape, a shelter for sheep and wet cyclists.

It acts as a beacon, a bearing, pointing further north to Shetland, aligning our outpost with another. A peculiar meridian to carry a message about a constitution at the furthest edge of the dominion.

As if blown to the edge by the elements, the words still cling tight to the etched transparency. There, the proposition is as anchored as in the seat of Holyrood, yet ephemeral as the Hebridean light. In Gaelic and Shetlandic they are resonant of Viking graffiti, cup and ring stone, wayfarers marks, pages from a missionary's rant.

An explanation of the design of the Scottish Parliament building

GEORGE GUNN, The Scottish Parliament, Edinburgh

A POEM writ large on a wall, on a corner so that the poem bends, might seem an unlikely starting point for a journey into representative democracy. But Angus Reid is no ordinary artist, and one whose fluid thought processes are stimulated by and in turn enrich the evolution of Scotland's political progress.

THE poem at the core of this creative project is, in form, a classic 14th century Petrarchan sonnet: 14 lines of 10 syllables. What Reid does is to divide each line into 7 and 3 syllables so that the poem can physically 'bend' around any corner where it is installed.

The work reflects a central motif used by Catalan architect Enric Miralles in his design of the parliament building in Edinburgh – for Scotland, the physical embodiment of representative democracy. Angus Reid has picked up on Miralles' use of an open hand, whereby the MSP's in the debating chamber become the dexterous fingers, and the forearm and wrist represent the real power of the people. This power comes from the land itself as signified in Edinburgh by Arthur's Seat and the Salisbury Crags. The main unfolding dialectic of Angus Reid's 'Call for a Constitution' is the five fingers on the hand (for right-handed people the left hand, the 'listening/thinking' hand), which relate to the 'five principles': 'the sacred', 'freedom of conscience', 'the gift of every individual', 'communities' and 'the land'.

Whether you agree with the poem, or disagree, or just want to participate, you are invited to leave a drawing of your left hand on the response wall beside the poem.

Reid also invites us, the viewer/participator, to create our own poem, to imagine our own constitution, to decide upon our own five principles. It is an intriguing and timely notion which has its origins in the 'peace and reconciliation' architecture of the French visionary Le Corbusier and the 'space and light' sculptures of Barbara Hepworth, as well as in the revelatory and inspirational constructions of Miralles himself. Angus Reid's question to us is, I remind you, 'What kind of country do you wish to live in?' This is an 'open hand' question which cannot be answered by the simplistic dichotomy of 'yes or no'.

What Angus Reid suggests, through his art, is that we undertake a journey into what it means to be a human animal in the modern world. Do not look for certainties on this journey for this is the territory of image, both abstract and clear, where meaning is fluid but where the image nonetheless insists upon meaning, political representation and consequence. For this is political art. The image is freedom and freedom is energy and energy is love and love is responsibility – as he writes in his poem: 'to care for the land/ and wherever/ the land has been abused to/ restore it'.

All of this is also education and education is a gift offered in an 'open hand'. At Caithness Horizons, Angus Reid explained to his audience he wanted to 'take the poem on a walk and see what happens'. It may be too early or indeed too grand to say that this is the journey to a revolution, but this fascinating arts project has the seed of revolution in its conception, and like revolution (and democracy) it depends upon people and their participation.

By way of Shetland to Orkney; from Sutherland to Uist; Dunbar to Dundee, you can participate: open your hand, make your mark, and think about what kind of country you wish to live in.

See if you can turn the corner, along with the poem, into a new world.

THE SCOTTISH PARLIAMENT, Edinburgh

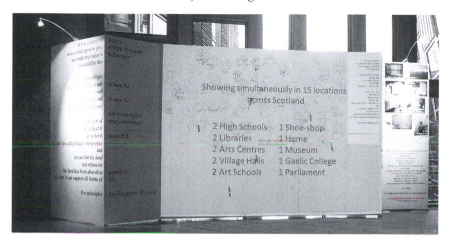

Showing simultaneously in 15 locations across Scotland

2 High Schools   1 Shoe-shop
2 Libraries   1 Home
2 Arts Centres   1 Museum
2 Village Halls   1 Gaelic College
2 Art Schools   1 Parliament

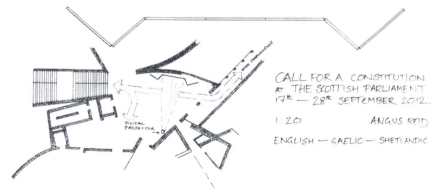

CALL FOR A CONSTITUTION
AT THE SCOTTISH PARLIAMENT
17ᵗʰ — 28ᵗʰ SEPTEMBER 2012.

1:20   ANGUS REID

ENGLISH — GAELIC — SHETLANDIC

Schools

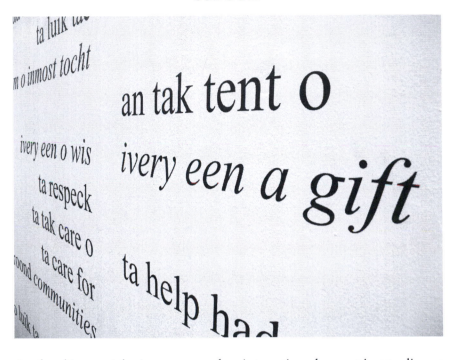

A school is a social microcosm, and an interesting place not just to discuss human values, but also to explore how they work. Also, schools are structures that mirror society at large: the majority of students are told what do to and how to behave by a minority that is in authority. A number of these schools simply wanted the installation, but two state secondaries asked me to go further and to create a charter written by students. The two poems are very striking: the first in St Thomas of Aquins High School speaks for all school-kids, and the second made with Stranraer Academy speaks specifically to their own school community. This created a series of interesting social challenges within the schools themselves because schools reflect the way that power structures either allow or resist democratisation, and seek either to hear or to silence the voice of the majority.

And here comes the cautionary tale.

In St Tams, the poem made it onto the wall, and into the heads of the senior pupils, but the next stage, the wish for it to be endorsed as a new school charter has remained undeveloped. Unable to organise a vote on their own, the project was left as an artistic curiosity rather than a blueprint for a better school and a new charter. Nevertheless, I am extremely grateful to the former head teacher, Grave Vickers, for understanding and supporting the project for as far as it got: it remains the only document of the kind of school community that students have defined for themselves, and is a potent gift to other schools.

In Stranraer the case has been long-drawn-out. The Stranraer poem made the St Tams kids jealous: it is cool and fast-talking, with an admixture of Ayrshire dialect. It gets straight to the point: students want 'two-way respect' from staff. The school resembles a factory with vast bare walls, and the best place for such a poem was, clearly, in the students' own handwriting to the full height of one of those walls. This split the Senior Management Team, and they needed the agreement of the Parent Council. Being a democratic body, the PC suggested putting the project to a vote by the whole school, and this excellent initiative was undermined by the Senior Management Team in a subtle way. Rather than simply vote for or against the poem, they demanded a three-way vote: for the handwritten version presented here, a printed version, or for none at all. 'None' narrowly won the most votes, even though the majority of the school had voted for the poem in one version or another, and the fact that nothing has happened since remains a problem. In a situation that is using democratic means to make a decision, surely the three-way vote should have knocked out the least popular option and left a clear two-way contest for a majority, as in a presidential poll? At the time of writing no response to this request for a second poll has been received from the school, although one is, herewith, politely requested!

It is our hope that the schools experience outlined here can continue to excite curiosity about these projects and their implications for school communities, and persuade others to try.

GRACE VICKERS, Formerly Head Teacher, St Thomas of Aquin's High
School, Edinburgh

Celebrating our Pupil Voice

St Thomas of Aquin's, Edinburgh was delighted to be asked by Angus
Reid to take part in the Call for a Constitution project. The S4 Modern
Studies class led the project through a series of discussions and
workshops to ensure that the charter was written from the pupils' point
of view, using language which meant something to them and the result
was a beautiful Pupil Charter which struck at the very heart of what
pupils wanted to express and was presented in the form a poem:

from an education we expect   friends
fun
new stuff
and   the right to a future
we expect to be able to show what
we're best at
and to become confident

we expect those that teach us to treat us
with respect
and with fairness
equalness
kindness
we expect   to be understood
to be given responsibility

and to be greeted by an open mind

and I expect you not to put yourself
above me
to treat me as you would wish
to be treated
to be non-judgemental

and then when I need it that you
stand up
for me just as I would stand up for
you

This was an important process for the school because it ensured that the charter was truly written from the bottom up and this poem was then displayed on the wall of the main staircase in the school and all pupils were asked to comment using their handprint to express their own responses. As a result there was an outstanding response to this initiative and all responses were shared in this display of hands.

Our pupils were clear that our school was a real community, much more than 'just about grades' and when faced with difficult situations we respond as a whole community treating everyone with 'respect, an open mind, and then when I need it that you stand up for me just as I would stand up for you.'

What was most impressive was that our pupils felt that they thrived when given responsibility and as a result grew in confidence and were eager to take on even greater responsibility so that they were able to make a real difference for the good of their whole school community. This also mirrored our whole school themes for the year: 'Everyone has a gift to share' followed by 'Let your light shine'.

In order to celebrate this important work, James Leckie (S4) and Andre Vitaliev (S4) were invited to take part in an event at the Scottish Parliament and also presented their poem at the whole school award ceremony. This was very well received by pupils, parents and staff and our parents were also invited to leave a handprint to express their response. So, from an education, our pupils have deeply felt expectations and an absolute commitment to showing that they are able to make a real difference to each other by living out their mission in practice to ensure, in real terms, 'the right to a future'.

PHIL ARCHER, Principal, Leith School of Art

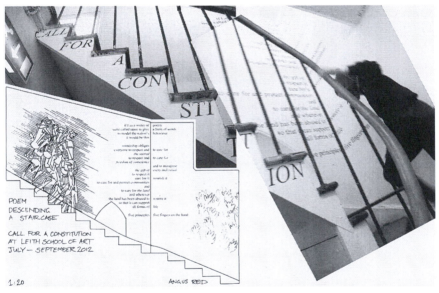

It was a privilege for Leith School of Art to provide the first wall for Angus Reid's 'Call for a Constitution'. As this project took off and spread throughout Scotland it fitted well with our theme this year of Connections. We felt connected to the parliament and the country and the debate on independence. We fully support the poem's focus on social, ethical and human values as opposed to petty politics. Our students showed their support by making handprints on the wall next to the poem – five fingers on the hand.

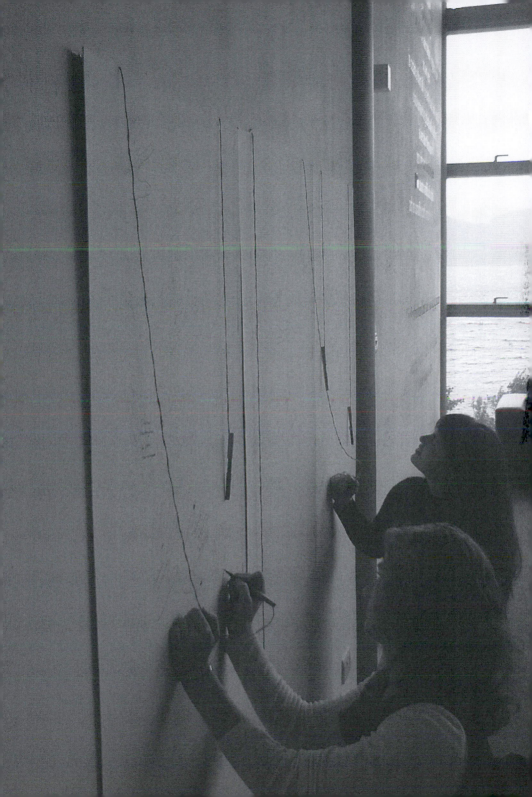

SABAL MÒR OSTAIG, Skye

LAURA SIMPSON, Duncan of Jordanstone College of Art and Design

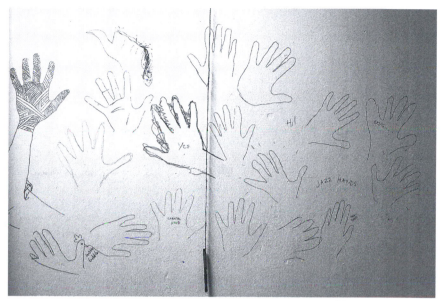

This project, built around the poem 'Call for a Constitution', stems from a personal quest to initiate a discussion around a constitution for Scotland. The project aims to move towards a contract between a people and a government built from the core question 'what kind of country do you wish to live in?'

The artist describes the poem as a 'marker that I hope can help to define a consensus'. For this reason the poem is as simple as possible and the words are there to be counted out on one hand.

The installation works with the architecture of the gallery space to deconstruct and highlight parts of the poem.

Bradshaw Art Space is one of several venues around Scotland, from Shetland to Edinburgh, in which the poem will be shown simultaneously, including the Scottish Parliament, where the poem will also be installed. In each venue the public is invited to interact with the installation, and this interaction will be represented in the parliament.

DAVID PROSSER, The Edinburgh Academy

The initial negotiations for the installation of the poem 'Call for a Constitution' on the walls of the classical façade of The Edinburgh Academy were not that easy. When Angus gets an idea, there is a determined drive that kicks in expecting all to follow, and for this project more so than any other, as core political values were the focus of his artistic attention. This project was going to happen, and with the passion of Bonnie Prince Charlie raising the clans, Angus expected others to put up their hands and follow. The possible implications of providing pupils with the implements of graffiti and the prime location of the front of the school on which to express their views were of trivial concern when there was a greater vision underway. Angus had faith in the maturity of the pupils to understand, appreciate and communicate articulately their viewpoint about an issue that should be central to all our common beliefs. He was 90 per cent justified: an impressive statistic in the political world, and a pretty impressive score in the world of education.

Angus spoke to the whole school at morning Assembly on National Poetry Day. It had everyone entranced and immediately caught up in the project. He spoke passionately about his vision with his usual verve and exuberance. He later expanded on this in a fascinating lunchtime lecture, which unfortunately had to be cut short by the unforgiving school bell. This was a real pity as he was just moving on to a section of slides describing Miralles' design of the Scottish parliament. The lecture theatre was packed and no one wanted to leave.

Some staff and pupils went to the subsequent debate in the stunning Committee Room 2 of the parliament building. To be part of this was especially exciting for those pupils who are interested in a career in politics and have strong views to express. The idea that 16-year-olds aren't of an age to have a viewpoint on such matters was completely disproved. They also got to see the final part of Angus's lecture and to experience what a truly exceptional building the parliament is. Following Angus's exposition of the ideas behind the design many people wondered why we are not more proud of this architectural masterpiece.

The installation of the poems in the school did look magnificent. On one side of the school hall main entrance the words appeared in English, and on the other Angus had found a meticulous translator in John Lister who had transcribed the poem into Latin. The deep grey vinyl lettering on the stone alcove walls gave the whole feel a real gravitas. It looked as if it was part of the original vision statement of the enlightened founders of the Edinburgh Academy. The pupils quickly filled a board with a web of handprints to show their support for the idea of a Constitution. The potential implements of anarchy were used for unity and the visual impact had the political weight that was part of Angus's vision. Politics can be a slow process but we hope that we will all get there in the end.

MATTHEW CROSS, Stranraer Academy, Dumfries & Galloway

S5 pupils at Stranraer Academy met with Angus to talk about their fundamental beliefs about the purpose and nature of school and the values which they felt should underpin their school experience. Angus used this to write a poem expressing their thoughts and feelings. This poem will be displayed in huge scale on one of the school's interior walls. The project has been very enthusiastically supported by the school's parent council.

I hope this poem will serve three major purposes. Firstly, it is a provocation to think about the fundamental relationships of school, the relationships between staff, pupils and parents and between individuals and the institution. As schooling moves away from an old autocratic model towards a model of teaching by consent, these relationships and the values they rely on require re-examination.

Secondly, I hope that the poem will make a bold statement about the importance of and value assigned to creativity in the school. To give a large and public place to this poem should be a strong signal to pupils that the school respects and encourages creative artistic endeavour.

Finally, I hope that the poem will encourage pupils to engage with the idea of a 'constitution'. Living in a country which has no constitution, the idea can seem very distant from young people, but in terms of understanding politics globally 'constitution' is a key concept – how could one understand the USA without a clear understanding of the idea of a constitution?

S chool is

bah T er

f R iends

grades an ' A that

and moneyat the e N d of the week

two way R espect

the e A s y part of life

Where they push you b E yond what you think you can do

respect you. respect them R espect you better

We are f A mily

no shouting C arrying on

we can A gree to disagree

Don't ju D ge me by the look I choose

you can E xpect me

in M ercury shoes

to be there to stand up for Y ou

POEM FOR STRANRAER ACADEMY   SCALE 1:50

The Past

Munitions workers WW1, courtesy
of the TUC Library collections'

CHAPTER THREE

The Past

MARY DAVIS

THE STRUGGLE FOR constitutional rights in the UK has been a long one – it is the longest in the history of western parliamentary democracies – and has served as an inspiration to many other countries and peoples. This section considers three essential lessons from that history: namely, how in England there appeared a fully developed democratic republicanism at the end of the Feudal period, and despite the violence with which it was crushed, how influential it has been throughout the world; secondly, how close Britain, like many other countries at the time, came to a socialist revolution 100 years ago and the factors that defeated it; and lastly the role of women throughout, and despite the concessions made to women in the past 100 years how the issue of equality has, and continues to be, fudged and avoided. If there is a theme running through these essays and the book as a whole it is the unwillingness of parliamentarians to concede rights to the population at large.

Introduction

There are few periods in history when the struggle between classes is so acute and evenly balanced that the ruling class is, for once, forced onto the back foot. The above named are two such periods, and these are partly explained by the fact that the economic and social gulf between the classes continued to widen dramatically in the mid 17th and in the early 20th centuries. Under such conditions of class polarisation, and a massive build up of grievances in the poorer classes (17th century) and later (in the 19th and 20th century) the fully fledged working class, a revolution developed in the 17th century and a massive strike wave developed in the 20th.

The English Revolution 1647 to 1649

The mid 17th century witnessed a revolution, usually misleadingly termed a 'civil war'; but if we consider that the ruling class could not continue to rule in the old way because the people would not let it (Lenin's definition), this is more than a civil war: the Royalists were defeated and Charles I was decapitated. But there is more: this revolution contained in addition a vigorous and historically unprecedented fight for a popular democratic Republic based on universal manhood suffrage. It is nothing short of amazing that this is not the business that standard histories choose to recount. However, one would have thought that the ideology inspiring these advanced ideas was well worked out beforehand, but according to Bernstein this is not so. Unlike the French Revolution, the ideas inspiring the English Revolution were a 'fugitive literature' that 'arose from the necessities of the moment.' That is not to say that when the radical thoughts of men like Overton, Walwyn, Lilburne and Winstanley were committed to paper in the ensuing pamphlet war of the mid 17th century they were ephemeral or peripheral – far from it.

The pamphlets circulated widely as did the Levellers' weekly paper, *The Moderate*, until it was suppressed in late 1649; and such literature had a profound impact on the ensuing rebellion. The Levellers emerged as a mass organisation in 1645–6 towards the end of the first English Civil War, which had witnessed deadlock between Royalist and Parliamentary forces. Victories at Naseby and Langport ensued once the New Model Army was organised under Sir Thomas Fairfax with General Oliver Cromwell as his cavalry commander.

In order to understand both the ideology and the practice of the revolutionary upsurge, we would need, as Christopher Hill, Eduard Bernstein, H.N. Brailsford and others have done, to study the remarkable campaigns of the most radical groups on the Parliamentary side: the Levellers and the Diggers (who called themselves 'true levellers') and their main spokesmen, respectively, John Lilburne and Gerard Winstanley. The two groups were divided doctrinally and theoretically: the latter advocating a communist programme to which they sought to give practical expression in 1649 by beginning communal cultivation of common land at St George's Hill near London and in other settlements in other parts of the country. They were forcibly evicted by local landowners with tacit approval from the army under the command of General Fairfax. The Levellers, on the other hand, expressed the outlook of men of small property, artisans, yeomen and husbandmen. The significant difference is that Leveller ideas took hold in the New Model Army, and by 1647 the Army had become the dominant power in the land.

The New Model Army was itself a unique creation. Never before or since had such a democratic fighting force existed in the UK. Perhaps unaware of the political consequences of their actions, Parliament had been forced by military necessity to model it on meritocratic lines and officers held their rank not by virtue of social privilege but through their own qualification as soldiers. Class divisions did not operate in the army as they did in society. Uniquely among the armies of the time the New Model could declare that it fought for principles, for liberties and rights, and this ethos lead to a strong bond of shared values between officers and men. And, if the egalitarianism of the army accounted for its success in battle, so the politicisation of the army accounts for the English Revolution. The critical moment came when it was treated not for what it had become, but for what it's masters (parliamentarians who had been debarred from holding rank) thought it to be – a mere mercenary army to be patronised and paid off. The settlement was – predictably – inadequate and the army, unified by common grievances over pay, refused to demobilise. It was, albeit briefly, no longer an army under orders, but a militant union of armed citizens. It was into this critical moment – the lull between the first and second civil wars when tens of thousands of men bore arms – that the Levellers, many of whom were serving soldiers, injected political organisation and an articulate manifesto.

The broad character of the politicisation is important: it opposed the ideology of the ruling order in that it was democratic with a wide suffrage, it was tolerant unlike the prevailing Presbyterian ethos, and it was anti-imperialist. It stands as the first template in British history for revolutionary action: how a movement can surpass the redress of specific

grievance and fashion itself as an instrument of social and political change.

The army elected their own spokesmen, two per regiment, known as Agitators. The Agitators had a strong agenda: initially they represented the demand that Parliament honour arrears of pay, but quickly they adopted a more radical agenda, in particular protesting, on principle, at the plan to send part of the army to invade Ireland. These Agitators conveyed the army's grievances to the Army Grandees, Cromwell, Fairfax and Ireton, and the ensuing standoff was dramatic and fast changing. It began with the establishment of a representative Army Council that brought the grandees to the negotiating table at a church in Putney in October 1647, and then, through a series of remarkable pamphlets makes a quantum leap in terms of revolutionary consciousness. It was at that debate that the Agitators put forward the demand for a comprehensive re-organisation of the state, 'The Agreement of the People'. They offered it as a new social contract between government and people, and it was in the words of the Leveller song 'The World Turned Upside Down' … (or almost) because it was so radically different from anything negotiated before or since.

The Agreement of the People demanded the dissolution of Parliament and sought instead to institute annual or biennial parliaments. The supreme authority of the nation should, it argued, be vested in a representative body of 400 members. Members were not to be eligible to sit in two successive parliaments; taxes and tithes should be abolished; equality of all before the law should be respected and trials should be heard by 12 jurymen freely chosen by their community; the death penalty was only to be applied in cases of murder; and finally they argued that imprisonment for debt be abolished along with conscription. This was the Leveller contribution to the abolition of the 'Norman Yoke', the hated feudal imposition of the Normans.

Key to their demands was the extension of the suffrage to all men, although excluding wage labourers. Notwithstanding their differences, both groups, Levellers and Diggers, agreed that wage labourers were unfree and hence should remain voteless. The Digger solution for this was the most radical: to abolish wage labour altogether. This attitude to wage labour by even the most radical groups was a reflection of the fact that 17th century England was pre-capitalist, and hence a proletariat did not yet exist. It was also a reflection of the fact that all who were dependent on their 'superiors' like servants, beggars, wage workers and others, could not be given the franchise because they couldn't be trusted to remain loyal to the radicals. Presumably, the Levellers applied the same faulty logic to women although thousands of them supported the radical cause, in England and in Scotland. In the latter country women, led as far as we know by Barbara Hamilton, were instrumental in organising mass resistance to the new *Book of Common Prayer* introduced by Charles I into the Scottish Kirk in 1637.

The political element in the army was so keenly aware of both the momentous nature of their demands and the need for proper legal accountability that every word of those debates was transcribed verbatim. Cromwell was not expecting The Agreement, and the first order of business was to read it aloud. His reaction to it – from surprise, to aghast resistance, to grudging concession – can be followed in real time over the first three days. These pages, that document the first expression of demands that would be reiterated by the Chartists, and later by the Trade Union movement, were hot political property and subsequent to the days of Putney they disappeared for 250 years, only to pop up again in the 1890s when decisive popular protest had put the same demands back onto the agenda. It is also a curiosity that only half the debate survives: the other half would tell the tale of Cromwell's false agreement with the Agitators to put The Agreement to a universal vote in the Army, the event of which he subsequently hijacked to make his counter-revolution, to assassinate the leaders or force them into exile, and through execution by lot, regiment by regiment, to purge the army of Levellers.

This ruthless and imperialistic strategy of divide and rule was designed to terrorise the army into submission, but it was prolonged, deeply unpopular, and regularly punctuated by Leveller mutinies. These culminated with the execution, on Cromwell's direct order, of three Leveller soldiers at Burford in May 1649 and mark the dawn of his military dictatorship – what Brailsford terms as a decade of 'Puritan Fascism'. The violence of the Puritan reaction, and also that of the subsequent Royalist reaction, is a measure of the drastic extremes that the ruling class required to contain demands that they saw as a threat to their social privilege. However, 'The Agreement of the People' was popular and well-known and remained a decisive point of negotiation for two years, and despite the persecution of its authors, was presented in increasingly elaborate and coherent versions to Parliament on two further occasions, in 1648 and 1649. And it says much for the extent to which the revolution had changed consciousness in society that on this last occasion a woman inspired other women. She was Katherine Chidley, who following Elizabeth's Lilburne's example (Elizabeth was John Lilburne's wife) flung herself wholeheartedly into London's radical politics to emerge as a leader of Leveller women. In April 1649 several hundred of them besieged parliament, demanding the release of the Leveller leaders from prison. In their second petition, which may have been written by Chidley, they justified their political activity on the basis of 'our creation in the image of God, and of an interest in Christ *equal unto men*, as also of a proportionable share in the freedoms of this commonwealth' (known as: Petition of Women, Affecters and Approvers of the Petition of 11 September 1648 to 1649). Emerging from the Anabaptist tradition, this was the first time that the collective voice of women's demand for equality is heard in the British political tradition.

In 1653 the Leveller leader John Lilburne found himself on trial once more. Again Chidley rallied to his defence, organising a petition to the Barebone's Parliament that reportedly garnered over 6,000 female signatures. The women boldly knocked on the door, but the house sent out one of its members, Praise-God Barebones, to persuade them to go away. Their persistence wore him down, however, so another MP was sent out. This anonymous member told them that parliament could not recognise their petition, 'they being women and many of them wives, so that the Law tooke no notice of them'. The extent to which the popular demand for 'Soldiers' Rights' had taken hold of the wider imagination can be gleaned from their retort: not all of them were wives, 'and therefore [they] pressed for the receiving of their petition, which if they refused they should know that they had husbands and friends and they wore swords to defend the libertys of the people'. As citizens had fought not as mercenaries for another class but for their own rights and liberties, they had created a constituency with which women could identify.

Chidley's date of death is not known and perhaps she died soon after this episode, since nothing more is heard of her, whether as religious writer, political activist, or successful woman of business. Brailsford tells us that women were active in collecting signatures for Leveller petitions especially in London. In this respect they, the Levellers, were ahead of their time – the Anabaptists always praised and supported equality and the vast majority of Levellers were Anabaptists. Lilburne regarded this as fundamental. He proclaimed the equality of all women and men, but also according to Brailsford he rejected distinctions of class and also the patriarchal family itself. This is a remarkable radicalism to find in any writing of the 17th century.

Although the influence of the Levellers was effectively eclipsed after Burford, Lilburne's personal popularity remained high. This was shown in October 1649 when Lilburne was tried for High Treason in the Guildhall. He defended himself and was acquitted by the jury against the recommendations of the judge. Joyful demonstrations were held in London and a commemorative medal was struck in honour of his acquittal.

Lilburne had remained radical and far-sighted. As Cromwell purged the Parliament of dissenters and pressed ahead with the trial of Charles I, Lilburne's was the only voice on the Republican side to speak out against the execution. The tragedy of this political/military manoeuvre by Cromwell can be seen in retrospect: Lilburne opposed the execution of Charles I on the grounds that the basis of the new republic had not been laid: the 'Agreement of the People' had not been ratified. Cromwell's commonwealth got off to the worst possible start, with no extension of the franchise and no commitment to representation. The wished-for transformation of society was shackled first by dictatorship, and next by restoration. It would take 250 years for a popular uprising to demand these changes anew and force them on an unwilling parliament. In the meantime, these ideas changed those parts of the world that were able to extricate themselves from the influence of the minority gentlemen's club, such as America and later France. Lilburne's clarity remains as critical today as it was then, and applies equally to the Scottish Referendum for independence: simply to topple one authoritarian system is inevitably to replace it with another if there is no agreed constitution already in place. Lilburne remained prescient and although his fears were realised, his foresight is still instructive.

We owe a great debt to those excellent historians of the left like Hill, Brailsford and Bernstein who have challenged the dominant Whig interpretation of British history and uncovered this rich seam of otherwise undiscovered radicalism. The Levellers were defeated physically, but their ideas were not; these ideas inspired Milton and later played a leading role in stimulating the American and French Revolutions. Hill attributes the work of an 18th century woman historian, Catherine Macaulay (among others), in passing Leveller ideas into the radical tradition of the 1760s and hence preparing the ground for the American and French Revolutions.

Although none of the historians cited above claim that the Levellers were an early socialist organisation, they all claim that the Levellers were 'the first modern broad-based activist political party in Britain' (Hoyle). It was organised down to ward and parish level in the City of London and in the home counties. The reality is that the Levellers represented the most widely socially supported but unrepresented political movement in the country, and that parliament wanted absolutely to exclude this influence. The suppression of the Levellers led to two and a half centuries of democratic disaster and it was the same call, for suffrage, for social justice and a new relationship between government and people that was

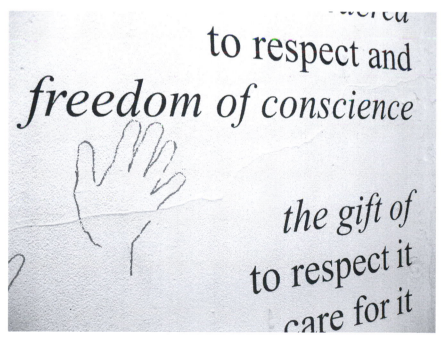

taken up by the Chartists in the 1830s, and in our modern industrial era in numbers that caused near-revolution in the years 1910–1914. Once again the ruling class were forced onto the back foot and sought the most extreme measures to suppress this voice.

The Workers' Story, 1910 to 1918

The Levellers were a movement whose solidarity was formed by mass participation in an armed force. Roughly 100 years ago, England, Scotland and Ireland erupted once again. These were not revolutions (although they nearly were). They were widespread revolts led by the class missing in 1647: industrial workers. In fact the revolts were so widespread that the name commonly attributed to them is 'the Great Unrest'. By the 19th century Britain was a predominantly industrial society with a large working class inhabiting major towns: all very different from the mid 17th century.

The revolts in the early 20th century were all the more surprising given that they occurred in the era of Imperialism, when the struggle for the domination of world markets was intense especially between the main imperialist powers: Britain, France and Germany. Nonetheless as we shall see Imperialism divided workers, and the ruling class were as fully aware of this as they were of the divisions based on race and gender. This prompts the rarely asked question: in Britain, where did women figure in the mass uprising that followed when the majority of them were workers?

Despite the attacks and difficulties meted out by the ideological and repressive apparatus of the state, trade union membership had grown to two-and-a-half million by 1910. The Lib-Lab approach of the parliamentary leadership, together with the class collaboration of some trade union leaders, led to growing discontent and frustration amongst the trade union rank and file. This was to result in the growth of syndicalist tendencies in many unions, a rejection of political parties, and the belief that trade union action alone was sufficient to resolve workers' problems.

From 1910 until the outbreak of war, the number of working days lost in strikes rose to an annual total of ten million or more, while membership of trade unions rose from two-and-a-half million workers in 1910 to four million by 1914. Major unions like the miners (MFGB), the Dockers and the Railway workers all staged strike action in this period. Although these strikes were defeated by the brutal action of government forces this did not deter trade union organisation and militancy. Within a year, the membership of the Miners Federation had leapt by almost 160,000 to over 900,000, making it at this time the biggest and potentially the most powerful union in the world.

In the summer of 1913, an industrial storm broke out in Dublin. The Irish Transport and General Workers Union, led by James Connolly and Jim Larkin, both of them Marxists, took on the might of the Dublin employers. The Employers' Federation had thrown down the gauntlet when workers on the *Irish Independent* were told to leave the union or face the sack. The printers chose to back the union and were therefore locked out. This signalled a general employers' offensive that led to a massive 25,000 workers being locked out by September. The employers had no qualms about using the full might of the state to crush the Dublin workers; meetings were banned and workers arrested, including Larkin and Connolly.

From the ranks of those picketing for the Transport Union, a workers' defence organisation was formed: the Irish Citizen Army. This force sought to counter the terror of police violence that had resulted in the murder of two workers and the wounding of 400 others in the course of the lockout. The Citizen Army was open to all militant workers, and was determined to defend the strikers and their organisations. In reality, this body constituted the world's first Red Army, and conducted its military operations under the flag of 'the Plough and the Stars'. Connolly had set up a rifle club to which his men contributed sixpence a week, from which guns were bought illegally from British soldiers in Dublin. Women helped to stitch and sew the Army's dark-green uniforms and later bore arms, and ex-regular army NCOs and reservists assisted in shaping the Citizen Army into an efficient fighting force.

'An armed organisation of the Irish working class is a phenomenon of Ireland', stated Connolly.

> Hitherto the workers of Ireland have fought as part of the armies led by their masters, never as a member of any army officered, trained and inspired by men of their own class. Now, with arms in their hands, they propose to steer their own course, to carve their own future.

The Citizen Army grew out of, and was organically linked to, the Irish Transport and General Workers Union. Its headquarters were in the union's Liberty Hall. It was in reality a weapon of the trade union movement fashioned to defend workers from the violence of both employers and state. It was an extension of the picket line. The workers therefore were not pacifists: they would fight with arms in hand if necessary to protect their rights and organisations. Sympathy strikes, involving some 7,000 British rail workers, were the tip of an iceberg. The mood of workers across Britain was disposed to fight alongside their Irish brothers and sisters. Unfortunately, the TUC failed to translate this widespread sympathy into a boycott of Irish trade, as many of its leaders were opposed to the policies and strategy of Jim Larkin. A special TUC in December overwhelmingly rejected Larkin's call for sympathetic strike action. Nevertheless, mass meetings were called to hear Larkin in Manchester, Sheffield, Glasgow and elsewhere.

By 1913–14 there were on average 150 disputes a month, but this figure does not do justice to the real conflict between capital and labour. The explosive struggle was on an even higher level than in the late 1880s and early 1890s (when unions developed amongst unskilled workers and women workers, and a wide range of strikes developed such as the matchwomen's strike of 1888 and the dock strike of 1889). It had a higher degree of aggressive militancy, sometimes violent and often unofficial in character. The fears of the ruling class were expressed openly in the capitalist press, and Connolly suggested that the most salient feature of the turmoil at that time was the general spirit of revolt, not only against employers of all kinds, but also against leaders and majorities, and Parliamentary or any kind of constitutional and orderly action. This indicates not only the growth of militancy, but a new creed within the ranks of the unions, namely syndicalism.

The philosophy of syndicalism had a powerful influence in these years. From 1900 to 1912, the social conditions produced by the impasse of British capitalism had pushed a whole layer of workers towards direct action and industrial unionism. Syndicalism showed absolute disdain for the antics of the Labour group in the Commons, which had become a mere adjunct of the Liberal Party. This disgust with Lib-Labism, viewed as embodying the worse kind of reformism, led to a rejection of party politics, and a concentration on industrial unionism and rank-and-file movements.

Another key plank of syndicalism was the rejection of 'official' leadership. This was most ably articulated in 'The Miners' Next Step' (1911), the platform of the Unofficial Reform Committee in the South Wales Miners' Federation. This platform, originally drafted by Noah Ablett, a Maerdy check-weigher, was born out of the miners' bitter struggles of 1910–11. 'Leadership implies power held by the leader', stated 'The Next Step'.

> Without power the leader is inept. The possession of power inevitably leads to corruption. All leaders become corrupt, in spite of their own good intentions. No man was ever good enough, brave enough or strong enough to have such power at his disposal as real leadership implies.

The aim of the Unofficial Reform Committee as a 'no-leader movement' laid heavy stress upon the need for unofficial action apart from the official movement. The proposals contained in 'The Miners' Next Step' created a furore in the South Wales coalfield, which soon spread to other areas. The old officials of the SWMF held up their hands in horror at these suggestions, and Labour leaders of all shades attacked it. While the syndicalist school pointed to the need for unofficial action, it tended to regard such action as principle, rather than as an alternative when the official movement acts as a barrier to struggle. The syndicalists tended to bend the stick too far in one direction as a reaction to the conservative role of the trade union bureaucracy. These ideas nevertheless found fertile soil amongst militant trade unionists, particularly the younger fighters, and in such bodies as the Socialist Labour Party, the Syndicalist Education League and the Plebs League.

As James Connolly, who worked as an organiser for the syndicalist

Industrial Workers of the World (IWW) in America, and who was also a member of the Socialist Labour Party (SLP), explained:

> [In] the light of this principle of Industrial Unionism, every fresh shop or factory organised under its banner, is a fort wrenched from the capitalist class and manned with the soldiers of the revolution to be held by them for the workers. On the day that the political and economic forces of labour finally break with capitalist society and proclaim the Workers' Republic these shops and factories so manned by Industrial Unionists will be taken charge of by the workers there employed, and force and effectiveness given to that proclamation.

However, Connolly later rejected this view. In 1908 he left the SLP and made the following hard-hitting criticism of its leadership (Daniel de Leon) and organisation:

> A socialist party that holds no meetings except during election times, that repeats like a parrot whatever is said by one man... that in a number of the largest cities in the country was not able to put up a ticket after 20 years of activity... such a party is... a fraud and a disgrace to the revolutionary movement.[1]

Syndicalism's rejection of leadership and concentration on 'rank-and-fileism', in reality, simply played into the hands of the right-wing leaders. Their fixation with the general strike as a weapon for changing society – which was a widespread view on the left – tended to ignore or under-estimate the nature of the capitalist state. They imagined that such a display of force during the general strike would result by itself in the collapse of capitalism. Such was the classic view of the Industrial Workers of the World (IWW) in the United States. This was a profound mistake. The theories of syndicalism, in its different varieties, reflected at this time a certain political immaturity of the working class. It would take the experience of the Russian Revolution of October 1917, which attracted the enthusiastic support of syndicalists worldwide, to clarify the way forward.

Nevertheless, syndicalism did provide the revolutionary focal point

---

1 Quoted in David Howell *A Lost Left*, p. 51, Manchester University Press, 1986

for the struggle of rank-and-file militants, especially in the rail, mining and engineering unions. In 1911, Tom Mann founded the Industrial Syndicalist Education League. A year later, the Amalgamation Committee Movement was established in the engineering industry to work for industrial unionism, reform of the ASE, and to promote workers' control. Rank-and-file Vigilance Committees were also established on the railways. Amongst the miners, the Unofficial Reform Movement was established. These movements helped to forge a number of amalgamations in the trade union field, especially on the railways and in transport. They also played a crucial role in the rise of the shop stewards movement during the war years and the left-wing Minority Movement during the 1920s.

Just prior to the First World War, splits in the Social Democratic Federation (SDF) and discontent within the Independent Labour Party (ILP), left-wing Clarion groups and others, led to realignment and the creation of the British Socialist Party (BSP). In early 1914, the BSP took the decision to affiliate to the Labour Party and seek a road to the politically organised workers. Militants in both the BSP and the SLP – people like William Gallacher (BSP), Arthur MacManus (SLP) and David Kirkwood (ILP), who led the famous Clyde Workers' Committee – played an important role in promoting industrial unionism throughout these years. These experiences were of fundamental importance in shaping the outlook of the shop stewards' movement right up to the formation of the British Communist Party in 1920.

In the years leading up to the First World War the militant mood in industry was far from exhausted. A whole series of new demands were being made by miners, transport, and engineering workers. In July 1914, all of London's building workers were out on strike. New political demands now came to the fore, such as nationalisation under workers' control of the railways and the coalmines. Under the pressures of the rank-and-file, a new industrial body came into being, embracing some 1,500,000 workers: the famous Triple Alliance, made up of miners, rail workers and transport unions. Such a potentially powerful organisation posed a deadly threat to the ruling class. For the workers it represented a qualitatively higher level of struggle than ever before.

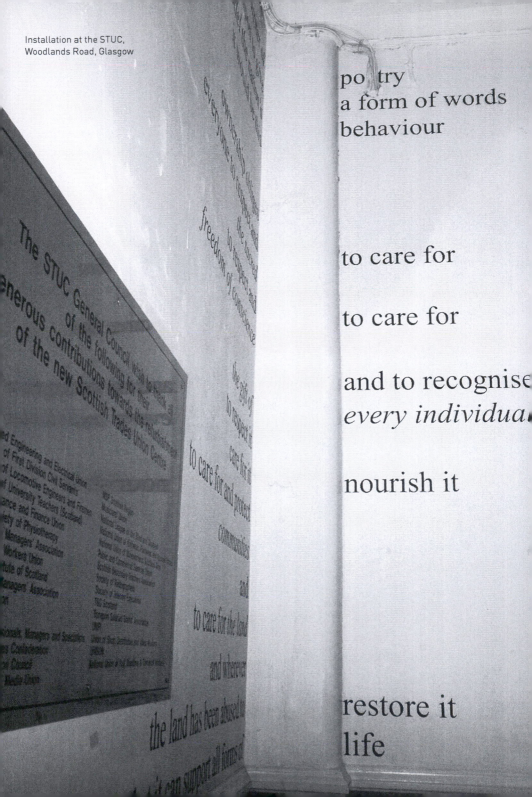

The STUC General Council wish to thank all
of the following for their
generous contributions towards the refurbishment
of the new Scottish Trades Union Centre

Every one to have the
freedom of conscience

the gift of
to respect it

care for it

to care for and protect

communities

and

to care for the land

and wherever

the land has been abused to

po try
a form of words
behaviour

to care for

to care for

and to recognise
every individua

nourish it

restore it
life

The growing crises in economy, in politics, and in international relations, were all symptoms of a general crisis of world capitalism. All were a manifestation of the fact that the system was reaching its limits, that the contradictions were intensifying, and that there was no peaceful way out of the impasse. As well as this international crisis, Britain was also consumed in a full-blown political crisis at home. The Liberal government was faced with an army mutiny in Ulster led by Sir Edward Carson ('the Curragh Incident') over its proposals for Irish Home Rule. Carson was, in turn, backed by a Tory-Ulster rebellion in Britain.

For the government, the threats of immanent civil war and revolution were extremely serious. Britain, by all indications, was heading for a social explosion. However, within a matter of weeks, the situation had been cut across by events for which the working class was totally unprepared: the outbreak of warfare on a greater scale than ever seen before, in August 1914. In other words, World War 1 extinguished the hopes for a progressive social settlement, and saved British capitalism.

For Women, 1914 to the present day

Women occupy a special position as an oppressed group in this story, and the following is an account of the bad deal that women have had in the successive settlements from 1914 to the present day, and is a rallying cry for solidarity under the banner of the women's charter.

Broadly speaking the issue of women's rights become visible only because the pre-war period marked the height of the suffrage campaign, and thereafter (apart from the campaigning work of Sylvia Pankhurst) it was considered to have fizzled out. This is a false perspective, and women continued to make a huge contribution to the workers' struggle. The disappearance of the issue may be explained by the fact that the leadership of the major organisation campaigning for women's rights, the Women's Social and Political Union (WSPU), was virulently opposed to the strike wave of 1910–14.

In terms of the participation of women in trade unions, there was an increase in women's membership by 1914, but 90 per cent of women remained unorganised. Any increase in membership was due to the work of the National Federation of Women Workers (NFWW) and to a lesser extent the Workers Union (WU) – the former had 20,000 women members by 1914.

So how do we explain the fact that women were still largely ignored and unorganised by the mainstream unions? Syndicalism (except in Ireland) was not interested in women, and 'the one big union' idea didn't encompass the small workshops in which women worked: laundering, dressmaking, jam making etc. The economic demands of the war changed this.

1914 to 1918

The war witnessed the massive recruitment of women into jobs vacated by men who had gone to fight. This was especially marked after 1916 when conscription was introduced. Women workers were drawn into the mainstream of the labour process and, to a lesser extent, into the labour movement during the war, especially because of the issue of *dilution* – a euphemism for paying women considerably less than the male workers they replaced. Women's trade union membership increased by about 160 per cent during the war, but only the National Federation of Women Workers and the Workers' Union were to make a serious commitment to organising women. By 1918 the WU employed twenty women as full time officials and had a female membership of over 80,000. This was more than any other general union and represented a quarter of the WU's own membership. There is little evidence, however, that the demands of women trade unionists, especially for equal pay, were ever placed high on any bargaining agenda during the war despite the fact that early on, in 1915, a conference called by the Women's War Workers Committee, drew up a comprehensive list of demands including the rights to training, trade union membership and pay parity.

The peak of women's trade union membership was reached in 1920 (nearly one and a half million, 25 per cent of the total female workforce). When the pre-war strike wave continued, this time it involved masses of women workers. At the same time the shop stewards and workers committee movement formed and was strong in many English and Scottish industrial towns. The issue which united male and female workers after 1914 was the question of class politics. This was partly explained by the fact that there had been a change in the character of male leaderships of trade unions – they were now more socialist and feminist orientated. The best example of this is James Connolly who argued in *The Re-conquest of Ireland* that 'the women's movement has synchronised with the appearance of women in the industrial field'. J.T. Murphy also spoke out against sexism, although the Sheffield Workers' Committee remained a male dominated organisation. In Scotland the Clyde Workers' Committee was reconstructed at the end of 1917 (influenced by the Russian Revolution) and its first action was to call a mass strike in support of four sacked women workers at Beardmore's factory.

This must be seen in the context of a broad strike wave that took root across the country. 1919 saw the most serious strike wave since 1910: 35 million working days were lost in strike action, six times as many as the previous year. These strikes included action by the police and armed forces, all influenced by risings in Hungary, Germany and Russia.

Unsurprisingly, when in 1918 the first Equal Pay strike occurred, it was initiated, led and ultimately won by women workers. This was the strike of women tramway workers, starting in London and spreading to other towns in the south-east, over the offer of an unequal war bonus. The strike also spread to the London Underground. Mary Macarthur, the Scottish Trades Unionist and Women's Rights campaigner described the strike as 'a landmark for the women's movement and for trade unionism'.

This successful tram and tube strike of 1918 resulted in the decision of the government to establish a special enquiry as to whether the principle of wage equality between men and women should be applied to all industries. The result of this was the Report of the War Cabinet Committee on Women in Industry. It concluded 'that industry is normally a function of the male, and that women, like non adults, are only to be permitted to work for wages at special hours, for special rates of wages.'

The Inter-War Years

The peak of women's trade union membership reached in 1920 dropped to a mere one million by 1939, despite the fact that the percentage of women within the total workforce had risen. There are several factors which can explain this bleak statistic chief among which were the attitudes of the unions themselves. In the general climate of unemployment, cost cutting and reversion on the part of the unions to narrow and sectionalist attitudes, women workers were perceived as a threat. Their employment was rising (from 27 per cent of the total workforce in 1923 to 30 per cent in 1939) at the expense, or so it was thought, of men.

This provoked two contradictory attitudes on the part of the male leaders, both of which were motivated by self-interest. On the one hand many unions which organised in industries with a high percentage of women workers (eg shop workers – Union of Shop, Distributive and Allied Workers, USDAW; teachers – National Association of Schoolmasters, NASUT; local government – National and Local Government Officers, NALGO; and post office workers – Union of Post Office Workers, UPOW) sought to restrict the employment of women by calling for a strict application of the marriage bar, or the introduction of one. Almost all of them refused to campaign or shelved demands for equal pay and instead pursued wage claims which increased the differentials between men and women. Others, like the UPOW in 1935, went even further and called for a halt to female employment altogether. In these ways many of the unions contributed massively to the problem that they thought they were addressing, namely the use of women as cheap labour in a time of recession and high unemployment.

On the other hand, the overall drop in trade union membership at this time was a problem that might be redressed if women could be persuaded to swell the declining ranks. Thus at the same time as pursuing negative policies on the employment of women, individual unions and the TUC were actively involved in recruitment campaigns. Trade unionism, according to a special leaflet adorned with a radiant looking female waving from a first class carriage, was the 'ticket' to health and beauty. Apart from the

STRIKE ON THE TUBE RAILWAYS

To Enforce Equal Pay for Women and Men.

Following the resumption of work yesterday morning by the great majority of the striking bus and tramway employees a new strike was declared last night by a meeting of men and women employed on the Tube railways. A number of Tube conductresses remained out yesterday, though the services were practically normal, as they were on the tram and bus routes, except in one or two districts, as, for instance, in the South Metropolitan Tramways area.

Last night's meeting, which was private, was held at the King's Hall, Walworth, and was attended by over a thousand workers, who discussed the question of equal pay for men and women. Mr. W. T. Foote presided, and the speakers pointed out that it was essential for women to be put on equal terms with the men as regards pay, especially in view of the position of discharged soldiers later on.

A News Agency representative was afterwards informed that a resolution had been passed unanimously deciding to cease work forthwith.

The Chairman said that this would mean that a strike would take place to-day.

CONTROLLER'S STATEMENT.

At an early hour this morning the Controller of the Underground Electric Railways in a statement to a representative of "The Daily News" said: "We believe that a section of the men at a meeting held last evening decided by a small majority to come out on strike in support of the demands of the women workers, but we have received no official intimation on the subject.

"In this course we understand the workers acted against the advice of their trade union, and that they refused to allow the representatives of their executive into the meeting. There was no trouble in the working of the trains last night, but we do not know what may transpire this morning."

G.W.R. WOMEN STRIKE.

Advice of Mr. J. H. Thomas to Resume Work Pending Negotiation Ignored.

Women workers employed at Paddington and Old Oak Common Stations on the Great Western Railway struck work yesterday, and last night they held a meeting at the Windsor Castle, Harrow-road.

Mr. J. H. Thomas, M.P., who addressed the meeting, advised a return to work pending the consideration of the whole question at issue by the Committee on Production. In spite of his advice, after a prolonged discussion, the women decided to remain on strike.

They are demanding an additional 12s. 6d. a week to bring their wages up to those of the men, and, in addition, any further increase which may be conceded as the result of the negotiations now pending.

STRIKE ON THE TUBES BEGINS TO-DAY.

Decision Last Night to Cease Work Forthwith.

EQUAL PAY DEMAND.

Another strike is threatened to-day—this time on the London tube railways.

Over a thousand men and women employees on the "tube" at a meeting at King's Hall, Walworth, last night, presided over by Mr. W. T. Foote, discussed the question of equal pay for men and women.

The speakers pointed out that it was essential that women should be paid equal terms with the men, especially in view of the position of discharged soldiers later on.

The proceedings were private, but it was announced later that a resolution had been passed unanimously deciding to cease work forthwith.

The chairman said that this would mean that a strike would take place to-day.

WOMEN CLEANERS OUT.

Between two and three hundred women in the Paddington (G.W.R.) and Old Oak Common cleaning departments struck yesterday, demanding equal pay with the men for equal work.

The strikers are demanding an additional 12s. 6d. per week to bring their wages up to those of the male employees.

At a meeting held last night Mr. J. H. Thomas, general secretary of the National Union of Railwaymen, reviewed the whole situation, and advised the women to return to work. In spite of this, however, the women decided to remain on strike.

In a statement made last night Mr. J. H. Thomas said:—

"This stoppage or any support of it, instead of helping towards a satisfactory settlement, is prejudicing our negotiations.

A BLIND LEAD.

"We are supporting, as we always have done, the claim for the same war wage for women as men, but to follow the advice that some are giving, that our efforts can be helped by these spasmodic stoppages, is to follow the lead of those who would bring the movement headlong to disaster.

"It is my proud boast that, strong and powerful as is our organisation, strong as is our claim upon both the Government and the public, we have never, and I hope never will, lose sight of our national obligations.

"It is because I am satisfied that the members in all parts of the country when they realise the issue, as I have put it, will take my advice, that I confidently look forward to an immediate resumption by those whose action has been too precipitate than wise."

Railway Clerks' Unrest.—There is said to be trouble brewing between the railways and their clerical staffs. The Railway Executive Committee refuse, it is alleged, to hear the Railway Clerks' Association on behalf of agents, station-masters and supervisory staffs, who are members of the association—a limitation which, it is stated, "cannot be excepted."

Bus Girls Back.—The great majority of the London bus and tramway car strikers returned to work yesterday.

fact that such male designed campaigns were grossly insulting to women's intelligence, they were also an abject failure.

The Second World War

The war accorded women workers a high profile. This did not mean that the state, in spite of some temporary concessions, had any intention of meaningfully addressing women's 'double burden' of home and workplace. An uneasy contradiction existed in the official mind between the obvious necessity to maintain war-time production on the one hand, and the desire not to destabilise women's role in the family on the other. It manifested itself in an unwillingness to ensure any lasting or general changes to the social order to meet the needs of working wives and mothers. Even the frequently cited provision of state day nurseries for working mothers, which was undoubtedly an historic initiative, was in itself the locus of intense ideological debate between realists like Bevin in the Ministry of Labour and the traditionalists of the Ministry of Health. Although the former appeared to win, as witnessed by the fact that 1,345 nurseries had been established by 1943 (compared with 14 in 1940), this did not represent a real victory for women workers. Firstly, it failed to satisfy the enormous demand or indeed to provide childcare for the duration of the mothers' working day and, secondly, it was always clear that this was a war-time expedient only. What the state provided the state could easily take away.

Apart from long working hours, the strongest and most frequently expressed complaint of women workers in this period was the fact that their pay remained on average 53 per cent of that of the men they replaced. Unequal pay was not new, but the overt injustice of it was all the more marked now that women had temporary access to the traditionally better paid all-male craft jobs. As in the First World War, women proved themselves capable of tackling 'unfeminine' work, but despite official encouragement and then compulsion so to do, this transition was strictly regulated. Agreements were signed between employers' organisations and trade unions permitting the temporary substitution of men by women in predominantly male jobs, and again these were known as 'dilution agreements'. The most common agreements permitted a phased introduction of eligibility for equal pay although the caveat applied to most agreements that women had to be 'able to perform the job without assistance or supervision' was a hurdle rarely passed. In the non-craft sector, there was not such a straightforward dividing line between the work performed by men and women. The employers' strategy was to insist that the women war workers in semi- and unskilled work were doing work 'commonly performed by women'. This meant that dilution did not apply and the argument for pay parity was a non-starter.

The attitude and strategy of the labour movement leaders on the question of pay, and indeed most other aspects of women's wartime employment, shows their lack of immunity from the prevailing patriarchal climate. Most unions in the craft sector did not admit women members. The largest of them, the Amalgamated Engineering Union (AEU), changed this policy in 1943, although it was not envisaged that this would be permanent. (It was.) In that year, the peak year of mobilisation, one in three engineering workers was a woman. As a consequence, women's trade union membership reached its highest ever recorded figure of almost two million in 1943, roughly a quarter of the total membership of TUC affiliated unions. Paradoxically it was the craft unions, like the AEU, which were the keenest on ensuring that women be paid the rate for the job on the simple argument that if the bosses could get away with diluting wages for women this would drive down the male rate when they returned to their jobs after the war. In the non-craft sector where the employers failed to secure 'dilution' agreements, the unions contented themselves instead with negotiating a separate national minimum women's rate, which was roughly two thirds of the male labourer's rate.

Unsurprisingly equal pay remained a burning issue throughout the war with local battles initiated by women themselves, but by the end of the war the campaign went off the boil as the government and the TUC concentrated their efforts on persuading women to return to their more traditional spheres of employment, with domestic service ranking high on the list of priority jobs. Trade unions and the Labour Party were influential during and after the war. Indeed the government's industrial strategy in war and peace depended on the close collaboration – if not the incorporation – of trade union leaderships. It is for this reason that their attitude to women acquires such significance, and there is little doubt that both wings of the movement had never jettisoned their deeply engrained patriarchal assumptions about 'a woman's place'.

1946 to 1976

Aside from the health service, a huge deficiency of Labour's social insurance scheme, unremarked at the time (and hardly commented upon by male historians since) was the effect that it had on women. The benefit system was firmly based on the notion that the whole of civil society was organised into family units with a male breadwinner at the head of each. Married women therefore were not entitled to benefits on the assumption that they were, like children, dependents of the male head of household. Even if they opted to pay their own contributions, they could only receive reduced rate benefit on the spurious argument that their expenses were lower. Wittingly or not, Labour fell for the capitalist ideological construct of the family wage that had been developed in the 19th century and which bore no relation to women's reality then, and even less in the inter- and post-war period when the economy was dependent on the employment of female labour regardless of marital status. Such state myopia in relation to women had a practical motivation in that the welfare system was far cheaper to administer if its benefits were only fully accorded to adult males, but it was also based on deep-seated suppositions that the place of women was in the home and that their entry into social production was secondary to their domestic responsibilities. The Beveridge Report was thoroughly impregnated with overtly sexist ideas on the 'place' of women and the role of motherhood.

Such assumptions were given a further ideological boost in the post-war era by the 'scientific' findings of the psychologist John Bowlby who popularised the theory of 'maternal deprivation'. He issued dire warnings about the harmful long-term effect on children and adolescents who received anything less than 100 per cent of their mothers' attention during the first five years of life. Apart from the impact that this had on female work patterns, the unchallenged acceptance of such views fed the truly reactionary Labour policy of closing the state day nurseries which had been opened to meet the needs of women workers during the war. This was a useful cost-cutting exercise, but there is no doubt that it was motivated by anti-feminist considerations.

Hence despite the undoubted merits of the welfare state in general, its benefits for women left much to be desired and indeed its family-centred orthodoxy did much to keep women locked into traditional subservience. The fact that the TUC readily assented to the Labour Government's decision to close wartime nurseries and decided by 1949 that equal pay was 'inappropriate at the present time' because of 'the continuing need for counter-inflationary policies', served only to show how much their thinking was in tune with the ideology of women's oppression and the ingrained ideology of the 'family wage'. In practice, the principle of universality was to apply only to the male half of Britain's population.

Despite government inaction, the campaign for equal pay continued after the war. By 1964 the Labour Party Manifesto called for a Charter of Rights for all employees to include 'the right to equal pay for equal work', and the TUC Congress in September 1965 followed this with a resolution reaffirming:

> ... its support for the principles of equality of treatment and opportunity for women workers in industry, and calls upon the General Council to request the government to implement the promise of 'the right to equal pay for equal work' as set out in the Labour Party election manifesto...

The Labour Party's election pledge may have been prompted by its desire to join the European Economic Community (EEC) so that it would be in compliance with the Treaty of Rome's clause requiring member states to adopt the principle of equal pay for women. However, the application was rejected and the Wilson government shelved the issue.

Equal pay might have been forgotten for another decade or two were it not for the action of women trade unionists, but this time in the private sector. In 1968, women sewing machinists at Ford's Dagenham Factory went on strike over a re-grading demand. Clearly this was not a case of women doing the same work as the men, although their argument was that it required equal skill. This led to a number of other equal pay strikes and the formation by women trade unionists and others of the National Joint Action Campaign Committee for Women's Equal Rights (NJAC-CWER). A huge groundswell of protest against government and trade union inaction began to manifest itself. In 1968, against General Council advice, an amendment to a motion on equal pay was passed which called for TUC affiliates to support any union taking strike action for equal pay. The TUC even held a one-day conference on equal pay in November 1968. Most unions by this time had declared forcefully in favour of equal pay and appeared to be keen to do something at long last for their women members. May 1969 saw a massive equal pay demonstration organised by NJACCWER. Barbara Castle, the Employment Secretary, in order to forestall further unrest, decided to introduce the Equal Pay Act of 1970. This permitted equal pay claims to be made by women in the public and private sectors if they were engaged in the same or broadly similar work to men. However, although the Act was passed in May 1970, it was not implemented until January 1976, thus allowing employers just over five years in which to make 'adjustments' to re-grade jobs in discriminatory ways and render themselves immune from the very limited scope of the new legislation.

Thus the long fight for equal pay was not over with the passage of the first Equal Pay legislation in 1970. What this act highlighted is that which had been apparent throughout the history of women's paid employment in the 19th and 20th centuries: namely, that the real cause of women's low and unequal pay is the issue of job segregation and the consequential undervaluing of 'women's skills'. However, while ideology decreed that women's place was at home, the labour market determined otherwise. The years following world war two witnessed a labour shortage. Then as now, increasing numbers of women workers (and especially married women) filled the gaps. Given the gradual closure of wartime nursery provision, the only solution to the conflict between the demands of paid work and the demands of family and home was the compromise of part-time work. The prevalence of part-time work for women is made to appear as a great concession by capital to enable women workers to perform their dual responsibilities. In reality it is nothing of the sort. Part-time work accounts for a staggering 44 per cent of female labour in Britain today – the highest by far of any EU country. Far from being a kindly concession, it is an important mechanism to enforce the maximum flexibility of the female labour force at the minimum possible cost – in terms of employment rights, job opportunities and pay – to the state and to capitalism.

1976 to the present day

The predicament that women find themselves today in is highlighted by the situation of black women workers. Surveys and experience show that black women experience an additional ration of inequality in the labour market, suffering higher unemployment rates, lower wages and poorer prospects than their white counterparts. The Labour Force Survey indicates that the unemployment rates for male and female black workers are more than double the rate for white workers. Black women workers are concentrated in particular areas of employment, and mostly in semi-skilled or unskilled manual jobs mainly in the private sector, at the lower grades and on the lowest pay. Black Caribbean women are roughly equally divided between the public and the private sectors and are the least likely to work part-time of any other group of women, black or white. Overall black women are more likely to work in the service industries, although Indian and Pakistani women are twice as likely as other women (black or white) to work in manufacturing industry, particularly textiles.

Once part of the labour force, black women workers continue to experience inequality, much of which is well documented. However, there is a reluctance to acknowledge its main cause: racism, both overt and institutional. This has been heightened by a number of government measures, particularly the Immigration, Asylum and Nationality legislation (2006) which requires employers to check on the immigration status of all their current and would-be employees. The failure to tackle racism outside the workplace has repercussions throughout society. The fact that racist murderers and attackers escape punishment, that the alarmingly high number of black deaths in police custody remains unchecked and that the subliminal racism of the mass media is largely unchallenged perpetuates a climate in which racism is tolerated at work and on the streets. The insidious ideology of racism can only be challenged when its existence, in all its forms, is recognised.

Economic disadvantage due to racism and sexism permeates not only the world of work but all other aspects of British society. Black women suffer disproportionately from the worsening social conditions experienced by the working class as a whole after continuous attacks, since 1979, on all aspects of the welfare state. In short, black women suffer a triple oppression based on race, sex and class. Whilst there is now some understanding of this triple oppression, there has been a tendency to adopt a mechanistic approach to it. Such awareness as has existed among predominantly white Labour local authorities, political parties and feminist organisations has failed to touch the average black working class woman, and hence the lack of any real progress in spite of some positive action initiatives.

Black self-organisation within the trade union movement has played a role in raising awareness of the persistence of racism within the workplace, and it has also led to some degree of visibility for black people in their own unions, and in the TUC and the STUC. However given that union density is higher among black people, and is remarkably high among black women, the progress of black people in their trade unions is extremely limited and a cause for great concern. More and more black women and black people generally are becoming suspicious of progressive political organisations and trade unions, which do no more than pay lip service to their concerns. To some this is proof that existing political and women's organisations are racist.

Black women will respond to, and work with, political organisations which understand and are willing to listen to them, to share their problems and to fight alongside them for the same goals. The challenge for us is how this can be achieved. Patronage, ethno-centrism and middle class moralism (each or all sometimes masquerading as leftist progressive politics), have resulted in further alienation and a trend to develop totally separate self-organised groups. The opportunity presents itself for the labour and women's movement to go to black women, to the organisations established by them and their communities and, from a socialist perspective, to learn of them and from them, and to open out the political debate on the real issues raised by them and in so doing to strengthen the struggle both here and abroad.

Although there was a temporary halt in the growth of women's employment in the early 1980s, it is clear now that women, now 50 per cent of the labour force, are a vital and permanent part of social production. However, the expansion of women's jobs (and indeed jobs of all kinds) is based on a much narrower range of employment, reflecting the chronic decline in British manufacturing industry. So, for women and for black people – already the victims of job segregation – the expansion of the labour market in the new millennium will mean more of the same: low paid and low status jobs, the majority of which will be temporary, part-time or casual. The preponderance of such contractual arrangements is frequently justified in the name of 'flexibility' and they are commended to women as being 'family friendly'. In fact the opposite is true. Uncertainty about a regular source of income, together with poverty wages and the lack of affordable child-care, increases the burden on women and perpetuates a cycle of deprivation. Women are twice as likely to be low paid as men. It is in this context that we must view governments' drive to get women off benefit and into work, a policy that would be laudable were it not clear that their intention is to maintain the status of women workers as a source of cheap labour. But we must also note that the growth of poverty pay (below the National Insurance threshold), 'has set a welfare time bomb ticking… Today's low paid workers are set to become tomorrow's pensionless elderly underclass…'[1]

In considering how to challenge this dire situation, we must pay urgent attention to the wages struggle – a struggle which, over the decades, has failed to embrace the aspirations of women workers, who still only earn around two-thirds of men's wages. Must women workers wait another 100 years to achieve this most basic of all rights?

Up until 1984 some excuse for inaction could be found in the fact that the law itself was deficient. The 1970 Equal Pay Act only permitted claims where the women were engaged on 'the same or broadly similar work' to that of a male 'comparator'. Quite clearly this had a very limited application, since so few women are engaged on 'like' work with men. Thus, the Act failed to get to the roots of women's unequal and low pay: the problem for the majority of women workers being that they are in 'women's work', and the victims of decades of job segregation. All research confirms that women predominate in a narrow range of occupations, including catering, cleaning, clerical, retail and repetitive assembly work.

However, in January 1984 the Equal Pay Act was amended largely due to the watershed equal pay case of Julie Hayward, a cook at the Cammell Laird shipbuilding yard in Birkenhead. In 1984, supported by her union GMB and many of her male colleagues, Hayward brought a claim for equal pay, arguing that her skills and qualifications as a cook were of equal value to those of some of her male colleague craft workers. The successful outcome of her claim and the solidarity shown across the movement was a pivotal moment in the trade union movement on

---

1 TUC The New Divide, 1995.

Merseyside and nationally. The amendment was forced on an unwilling Tory Government as a result of trade union pressure and a ruling from the European Court. The amendment provides another and very important criterion for claiming equal pay. Now claims can be admitted if it can be shown that the value of the work a woman does is the same as that of her male comparators. The law does not lay down hard and fast rules as to how 'value' is to be determined, but mentions the possible use of such factors as effort, skill and decision-making. This new principle of equal value is of major significance.

Some unions are grasping the importance of equal value to a greater or lesser extent, but the majority of TUC affiliates have not considered a strategy, let alone pursued any claims. The net result is that the labour movement has an appalling record of under-achievement when they represent women workers, and pay differentials between men and women in this country are among the highest in the EU. There is a tendency, however, to presume that the situation can be resolved by a wave of the legislative wand from Westminster or from Strasbourg. Of course, this simply will not happen. Change for women workers will only come about through the determined efforts of our own trade unions. It is important to show that the ensuing push for equal wages, while initially benefiting women, will not disadvantage men. Quite the contrary, it is never in the interest of men to tolerate a permanent pool of cheap female labour. This only serves the general tendency of capital to reduce the value of all labour and thus to push all wages down.

Conclusion – a socialist perspective

We have tried to show thus far that the basis of women's oppression is class exploitation. Hence the challenge to oppression, like it or not, can never be neatly confined, but always has wider implications within society as a whole. Women need allies, both from other oppressed groups and also, most importantly, from the working class whose basic objective interest lies in challenging class exploitation, the root of all oppression. Socialists have a special role to play, and in two areas in particular.

Firstly, socialist women must work to build a broad-based women's organisation capable of challenging male supremacist ideas and practices, and to campaign on the kind of issues raised by women in the labour movement based around the Charter for Women.[2]

Second, socialists have to ensure that the labour movement itself takes up the issues raised by women, not as an optional extra but as an integral aspect of every agenda. This means that the fight currently being waged to ensure women's representation at all levels of all labour movement organisations is successful and that trade unions take up the demands of the Charter for Women, and continue to pursue them vigorously even when the climate is hostile.

This task assumes greater clarity in Tory Britain, 100 years on from the movement inspiring the Great Unrest. Today, the Con-Dem government is attempting (and succeeding) to solve what it deems a financial crisis, at the expense of the working class. Now as then, the rich are getting richer. Women in particular are suffering greater burdens than ever as a receding Welfare State and National Health Service impact particularly severely on them. In addition public sector jobs are being decimated, and this is the sector where the majority of women work. In short, what we are witnessing in Britain today is what has been called the 'feminisation of poverty'. Working class women in 1913 faced the main burden of the assault and in 2013 the same is true. The main difference between now and then is that in 1913 the ruling class was challenged by a powerful labour movement; today, although numerically stronger, the labour movement is divided, although the women's movement is not.

It is axiomatic that such a project involving the mass of working women will have profound repercussions for all aspects of democratic endeavour, for an extension of constitutional reform, for the struggle for equality, and for an extension of the rights of workers, male and female. The question of rights is a crucial one if the right to vote (comparatively recently won) does not remain a sterile victory. It must be international

---

2   See http://www.charterforwomen.org.uk/

in outlook and link with every progressive movement and where appropriate, share its values – be they ethical, campaigning or stand-alone. Wherever people are in struggle women must show the way as leaders.

poetry
a form of words
behaviour

to care for

to care for

and to recognise
every individual

nourish it

restore

life

five fi

Considering a
Constitution

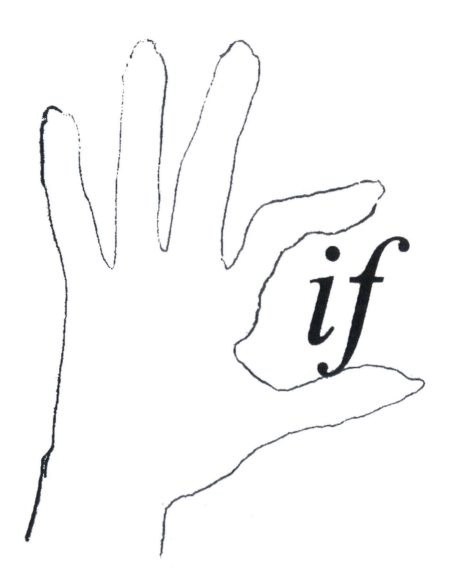

CHAPTER FOUR

Considering a constitution

Considering a constitution: a socialist view

JOHN HENDY QC

A CONSTITUTION IS no more than a set of rules which usually have special procedures to change them, making it more difficult to do so. Most organisations have constitutions but below we are talking about the constitutions of States. The constitution of a State usually sets out some fundamental rights as well as the architecture of government and law-making within the State. The Constitution of South Africa 1996 is a classic model constitution.

Though the UK is not unique, it is very unusual in having no written constitution. It is said to be a parliamentary democracy, meaning that everyone has the right to vote, the government is appointed by the majority of elected MPs in the House of Commons, and Parliament makes the laws. This description is, of course, a gross distortion of reality. Though nearly everyone has the right to vote, the first-past-the-post election system for MPs means that it is next to impossible for small parties to get a place in Parliament which is thus dominated by the two big parties. Since the subversion of the Labour Party by New Labour (which has all but crushed democracy in its own constitution) working class electoral choice is confined to differing shades of neo-liberalism (save for some notable individuals). In consequence millions feel that voting makes no difference and so do not vote. The big parties therefore focus on policies thought to be attractive in the 'swing constituencies', ignoring policies focussed on the working class. Democracy is further distorted by the almost unbridled power of the media (exercising its human right of free speech) which represents in an endless torrent what is to be valued and what is not in society. Few can remain impervious to the stream of propaganda and misrepresentation, particularly that effected by suppression of all contrary perspectives.

Within Parliament itself the House of Commons has been rendered almost (but not quite) toothless by the adoption by all governments over the last 35 years of a presidential style of government in which the possibility of influencing policy is confined to those who have exhibited consistent loyalty to the leadership. The House of Lords is undemocratic in a different way, full of government party appointees (replacing the feudal peers). Curiously, the House of Lords, replete with those who *have* climbed rather than those who still seek to climb the greasy pole, is more independent than such a moribund and undemocratic institution might appear.

Finally in relation to the UK's constitution, it is to be noted that though most laws are made by legislation, there are still small but significant areas of law-making (e.g declarations of war) which may be executed by Royal Prerogative – meaning, not that the monarch has any discretion in the matter, but that the government can make such laws without reference to Parliament.

The absence of a constitution (and a constitutional court) in the UK means that the courts cannot declare legislation unconstitutional.

Without doubt the presence of a constitution would be beneficial in restraining the dictatorship of the UK's present governmental system. A constitution for Scotland is proposed, no doubt a good thing. But three questions always arise. What provisions are to be contained in the constitution, who is to draft it and by whom is it to be approved?

All three questions are obvious but the last two need no comment from me. As to the first, others have noted that the constitution of Kosovo contained a commitment to membership of NATO. If the Scottish constitution did likewise it might prove impossible to ban nuclear weapons from Scotland as many wish. Likewise the Kosovo constitution contained a commitment to a market economy. This might not prove an empty slogan if the Scots constitution contained similar words and there was a constitutional challenge to nationalisation of the Grangemouth refinery, were it threatened with closure again.

The presence of a constitution, no matter how progressive in form and substance, is no guarantee of democracy, rights, and, still less, equality. Courts (including constitutional courts), governments, foreign powers and corporations can run rings round constitutions as we have seen so many times in the last hundred years or so. The interpretation of the US Constitution depends on which party appointed the majority of members of the US Supreme Court. Governments have subverted constitutions on dozens of occasions, most spectacularly in Nazi Germany. Foreign powers have engineered the overthrow of constitutions the world over well before and long after the Pinochet coup in Chile, all done without direct invasion. And corporate power subverts constitutional democracy across the globe. But those risks are no reasons not to have a constitution.

But even with goodwill, constitutions are limited in their effect. The Constitution of South Africa with its entrenched Bill of Rights and a committed, admired and liberal Constitutional Court has not managed to enforce the constitutional social and economic rights, the existence of which, it might have been thought, would lead to the eradication or at least diminution of the economic apartheid that continues to make South Africa one of the most unequal societies in the world. That too is, no reason not to have a constitution.

The truth, proved by history, is that progressive objectives and policies, whether contained in a constitution or not, require working class solidarity and mobilisation both for their attainment and for their continued application.

Constitutions are often written in one age and applied in a later one. In order to remain relevant they must be adapted and extended to deal with modern circumstances. Hence the doctrine of the 'living instrument' which has been so successful in evolving and extending the rights protected by the *European Convention on Human Rights*. Thus it is that notions of equality now are very different to that enunciated in constitutions and declarations of human rights 100 or 200 years ago. But courts with the power to adapt constitutions also have the power to pervert them. Though philosophers seek to find the holy grail of fundamental principles from which the ultimate bill of rights may uncontroversially be drawn; and religion, dignity, compassion, solidarity or equality may supply the answer for some scholars, the extrapolation of precise rights (or structures of democratic government) from such broad concepts is rarely uncontroversial. That problem is equally true of constitutions founded on socialist principles.

In Europe the *European Convention on Human Rights* is recognised by all 47 States of the Council of Europe, most of which States have constitutions which echo the *European Convention*. The latter establishes fundamental human rights which have been in effect for 60 years, administered by the European Court of Human rights. Yet the British government wishes to be rid of both Convention and Court on the spurious context that Britain does not wish to be dictated to by a 'foreign court'. If that were a legitimate reason then the Court and the Convention would collapse since the former, being composed of one judge from each of the 47 countries, is a 'foreign court' to all of them. The real reason is, of course, that the present UK government wishes to be free to violate fundamental human rights without being answerable for it – as the recent torture and rendition cases have shown. The *European Convention* is not, of course, part of the UK constitution; but does anyone seriously imagine that the British government would be any more respectful of human rights if it was? That is not, of course, a reason not to have a constitution including such human rights.

Even where human rights are clearly prescribed, courts, if so disposed, ignore them or abuse them. The Court of Justice of the European Union (the other Europe, 27 States in a common market of free movement of capital, services, business and labour) in the *Viking* and *Laval* cases overrode the right to collective bargaining and the right to industrial action which the European Court of Human Rights found to be essential elements of the freedom of association guaranteed by Article 11 of the *European Convention*. The decision of the EU to 'accede' to (sign up and be bound by) the European Convention has not led to any change in the caselaw established by *Viking* and *Laval*.

Human rights provisions may conflict with each other. If so the discretion to resolve the conflict rests with courts. In 2013 the Court of

Justice of the European Union relied on the right to conduct a business contained in Article 16 of the *Charter of Fundamental Rights of the EU* to allow an employer to break the obligation in the contracts of employment of workers it had taken over on an outsourcing to have their terms and conditions determined by national collective agreements. The workers' rights to the benefits of collective agreements protected by other Articles of the *Charter* (and by the *European Convention*) were conveniently overridden.

Under the guise of austerity measures, the Troika (the European Central Bank, the European Commission, the International Monetary Fund) have been undermining collective bargaining in EU States where the Troika has leverage. In Romania the percentage of workers whose terms and conditions of employment were protected by collective agreements fell from 98 per cent to 36 per cent in the space of some 19 months in 2011–12. In the UK 30 years of neo-liberalism has reduced the level of collective bargaining coverage from 82 per cent to 23 per cent, the second lowest level in the EU. All this is in spite of the obligations on States to promote collective bargaining which are set out in various international and European human rights treaties which those States voluntarily ratified and by which, in law, they are bound.

Short of socialism, the right to collective bargaining is the only way to address the problem of the falling real value of wages, which suppresses demand and hence inhibits investment and growth. It was the instrument of choice for reconstruction after the First World War (see the Whitley Committee)[1] and for dealing with the economic slump at the beginning

---

[1] JH Whitley chaired a committee in 1916 in the Ministry of Reconstruction which proposed voluntary Joint Industrial Committees for collective bargaining in each industry in which they could be organised, and statutory Wages Councils where they could not. The system declined in the early 1920s but blossomed again in the 1930s after the Great Depression. By 1947 87 per cent of British workers were covered by collective bargaining; by 1960 there were 200 JICs. Thatcherism smashed a structure which had given rise to Britain's most equal decade, the 1970s. See further: KD Ewing and J Hendy, *Reconstruction after the Crisis: A Manifesto for Collective Bargaining*, Institute of Employment Rights, 2013.

of the 1930s. Collective bargaining is also the only viable means for reversing the growth of economic inequality which is so disastrous for all levels of human society (as Wilkinson and Pickett have shown).[2] It is also the only workable way of achieving some degree of workplace democracy, and of doing something to alleviate the imbalance of power between the worker and the employer, the gross abuse of which leads to insecurity and zero hours contracts.

This leads to a fundamental problem with modern constitutions; short of socialism they simply cannot control the distortion of the human condition which is the result of neo-liberalism. It is hard to see how a Scottish constitution could have prevented the slashing of wages by and the extraction of millions of pounds in grants to Ineos, under threat of its closure of Grangemouth without the political will to nationalise the plant – a measure which did not need a constitution. But perhaps a constitution which gave real economic sovereignty to Scotland might have made a difference. The real problem is that nation States can be played off against each other in a global market for labour, commodities and capital. The power of transnational capitalism is today infinitely greater than when radical constitutions were drafted 100 years ago (such as the German Constitution of 1918).

As discussion about a constitution runs on, governments surrender to the corporations powers which should be exercised for the citizens and under their democratic control. The *Leveson Inquiry* (in which I appeared for the NUJ) revealed the extent to which Labour and Coalition governments had private meetings and made private arrangements with media tycoons. By the same token it is revealed that £20 billion worth of contracts for public services are awarded annually by the Coalition to private contractors thus effectively curtailing democratic control. This is set to rise to £100 billion in 2015. Of the £20 billion currently spent, two companies, G4S and Serco, both currently under investigation by the

---

2 See *The Spirit Level: why equality is better for everyone*, by Richard Wilkinson and Kate Pickett; Allan Books 2009, Penguin Books 2010.

Serious Fraud Office, hold £9 billion's worth of contracts. The existence of a constitution might not succeed in preventing the loss of public control and public ownership by outsourcing public services; but that is no reason not to attempt to prevent it by means of a constitution.

But on the wider stage there are moves afoot which the existence of a constitution could not restrain. The proposed *Transatlantic Trade and Investment Partnership* currently being negotiated between the EU and the USA is a mechanism to reduce the regulations (i.e. laws) on business to the lowest level tolerated by either party. By and large that means de-regulating such matters as environmental and health and safety protections in the EU to the low levels in the USA. There may also be a de-regulation of some financial and banking laws in the USA to the lower EU levels. The TTIP is also planned to prevent new regulatory differences emerging. This means that a proposal for improvement of European regulation could not be made unless the USA approved it. The surrender of democratic control is apparent.

Without doubt those who are masterminding the TTIP also intend to prevent any regulatory difference arising by the action of an individual State within the EU. The consequential loss of democracy within a State becomes obvious. Of course, to an extent this is already happening within the EU by the adoption of regulations and directives which bind all States. Whilst those which raise protection for consumers and workers are welcome, those which have the effect of requiring the privatisation of rail, postal and health services etc. are not.

The key players in the so-far secret negotiations for the TTIP are the European Commission and the twin lobby groups of the US Chamber of Commerce and BusinessEurope, a consortium of the major European business interests. They propose that such lobby groups should have the right to be consulted and participate in the negotiations for every kind of proposed regulatory change – prior to democratic and public debate. So business will influence the drafts before the public is even aware of the proposal.

More alarming still is the proposal that the TTIP should incorporate an 'investor state dispute settlement mechanism' which would in effect provide a court for transnational corporations to sue governments which have laws which adversely impact on their profits.

So far as worker and trade union rights are concerned it is easy to see how the TTIP will involve itself to attack all provisions said to create obstacles to trade or investment or said to distort the market or which entail a greater burden than equivalent measures in the USA. Thus we can envisage an attack on existing rights in Europe whether these are protected by national legislation or national constitutions or by the *European Convention* or by other international provisions such as the International Labour Organisation.

It is particularly significant that the TTIP does not provide for the incorporation of the rights protected by the *European Convention* or preserve its jurisdiction over human rights violations in Europe. Neither does the TTIP currently provide that all parties and all regulations must abide by the minimum standards set by the Conventions of the International Labour Organisation (and elaborated in its jurisprudence). The absence of such provisions makes a clear statement about the lack of commitment to fundamental human rights of the USA and the EU and their lack of leadership in the world in fundamental human rights standard setting. Part of the problem is that the USA has ratified only 14 of over 190 ILO Conventions and only two of the eight 'core' Conventions. It has not ratified the two most fundamental ILO Conventions, Nos. 87 and 98 on trade union autonomy and collective bargaining. At the same time employers' lobbying groups are seeking to downgrade the ILO by, for example, arguing that the right to strike recognized by the ILO for 60 years should no longer be recognised.

The Scottish constitution will have a lot of work to do. None of the above provides reasons for not having a constitution with, amongst other things, strong obligations to uphold human rights. But it must be clearly understood that only working class solidarity and mobilisation will provide a suitable constitution and maintain its effectiveness in protecting their rights and interests.

care for it ours

communities

and wherever

Considering a constitution: A view from a former Government insider

ALEX BELL

The idea of this book is lovely; a poem that expresses the values of a people. What is a written constitution if not something poetic which floats between the law courts and the soul – as solid as stone, as light as words?

Is 'light as words' right? 'Light as day' maybe?

We discussed holding a national competition for schools, or anyone, in which people could submit the opening lines of a constitution. The idea was to encourage a wide debate on what kind of society we value and on the difficulties of writing this down. Other things came along and the scheme was forgotten.

Perhaps 'light as air'?

All writers struggle over their opening paragraph, whether hacks or greats. The author looks up the page at the first set of words, as if it were mirror being smudged and needing a polish. Ultimately the writer must settle on a version. There may still be traces of dirt on the glass, but it will have to do.

No one else need know the words aren't perfect. They'll decide for themselves and move on, or forgive and read on. Any crimes will be committed on the language and the ear of the reader. In journalism the final copy will be marked 'stet' – let it stand – though it will fall within hours to be replaced with something else.

A constitution is different. The words cannot be polished later. They must stand for centuries. There is no looking back up the page once the ink is set, only in regret.

The discussion about a written constitution is simple up to the point of what it would say. Do we want a written constitution? Yes. Why? To protect human rights and a sense of the common weal, that the people are sovereign over excessive wealth, unfairness or extremism and could legitimately resist the effect of these.

The SNP has a long tradition of wanting a written constitution, a claim supported by the good work of a number of lawyers within the party and influenced by the intellectual merit of the case across all nations. It is both the right thing for Scotland, and the right thing for modern states international in outlook.

The European Human Rights Convention was incorporated into the 1998 Scotland Act, which established the parliament. As this is the fundamental document giving legal identity to Holyrood, and would remain so after a vote for greater powers and before a new constitution had been written, Scotland would start with a code on human rights enshrined in statute.

With the EHRC as part of the founding Act, it means all legislation developed in the parliament must abide by it and, should the EHRC itself develop, the parliament would have no choice but to amend any statute accordingly.

Some see this as unnecessarily restrictive and argue for Scotland to be a signatory to the EHRC but not to have this enshrined in the workings of parliament. This would bring Edinburgh into line with most other European capitals, who can challenge and debate changes to the EHRC without having automatically to follow them.

As the civil service is full of lawyers, it was impossible to get a common agreement about aspects of a written constitution. For example, important to the Scottish Government's case was that Scotland had a tradition of sovereignty of the people. In short, the people are the ultimate power.

This is said in speeches and debates as an indication of our historical attachment to democracy and justice. However, it raises complex issues.

If the people are in charge – and the courts, parliament and head of state merely functionaries of the people – then who owns the constitution? Clearly the people do, but how do they enforce or change that constitution? Which, between parliament and the courts, is superior in reflecting the will of the people?

Some lawyers said this was easily accommodated in the constitution and governance of the country, others that it raised nuanced points. Not having a legal training, I take the view it may yet have a critical influence on the writing process.

Then you must decide what kind of constitution – to simplify, a detailed one or one based on broader principles. The former ran the risk of requiring frequent referenda if major changes were to be made, the latter a pay cheque to lawyers who wanted to argue the toss.

The recent experience of Iceland, which had conducted a popular, open access process of writing the constitution, overseen by citizens, is very appealing. This seems to match the essence of sovereignty of the people.

These are some of the technical concerns. Equally important is who does the writing. I am clear the process should not be captured by Scotland's elites.

Modern Scotland, while it talks a good game about kindness, radicalism and equality, it is really a conservative place. Like most societies, it likes the familiar and is suspicious of change. Unlike most 'new' nations, it has already a lot of institutions. These are secretive by nature.

Devolution has not ushered in a revolution of the common man, but has entrenched existing power networks. You can get a lot done in Scotland with only a small contact list. Take a look at our current debate on powers. The same people appear first as individual experts, then as representatives of think tanks, then as advisors to parliamentary committees. We have a lot of job titles but only a handful of public participants. Those heard from are comfortably within the world's one per cent of wealth. It is time for the 99 per cent.

To have a genuine nationwide conversation about this, with citizens well informed, would require a degree of honesty and transparency which would threaten a lot of people, and take a long time. In this, the challenge is similar to that of having a sensible debate about powers.

The so-called constitutional debate has been going on for decades, heightened since 2007 and intensified from 2011. It is clear this is not enough. People feel ill-informed and that is a concern.

We have to face up to the one of the issues of our time – people do not engage in detailed debates and they don't trust politicians or official processes. How do we involve the community, and develop policies to protect the community, if the community doesn't want to listen, or is easily put off by superficial spats?

We then have to tackle the difference between voters and the community. Voters tend to be older and better off. That is why our unsustainable pension regime will continue for a while yet. People who vote are either collecting or about to collect their pension. The community pays for the pensions, and other services, but is not in the habit of voting. Scotland's future, and any process of writing a constitution, requires voters to think more about the community, and for the community to become involved.

A written constitution is an expression of the pact between citizen and state. That relationship is weaker than ever. We must guard against the document satisfying the 20th century desire for statements and not accounting for the changing relationships of the 21st century.

A constitution presumes a sovereign state. Sovereignty once carried weight, like a stone in the hand. It was a thing of substance. This is no longer the case. As I write there are rumours that the UK government is preparing to take the Guardian news organization to court over its expose of spying by Washington and GCHQ on us, the citizens of the UK, and on the citizens of Germany, France and other major allies.

What value sovereignty when the rights of a Berliner are as nothing to the fidgety ambition of a US official or a UK government keen to play catch with the American ball? If Germany, the heart and mind of the European continent, is not safe, then what chance Scotland?

In reaction to the Edward Snowden story revealing the depth of American and British abuse of human rights in the form of spying, the UK Foreign Secretary said no one in the UK had anything to worry about 'if they had done nothing wrong'. It rides through the right to privacy and takes us close to the assumption that all are guilty before being found innocent.

The relationship between any community and the global interest is clearly more complex and vital than at any stage in history. Constitutions of old had to define rights within a set of borders. This is no longer enough and any document aiming to express the will of a people must articulate how this functions in a borderless world.

We can see the formation of a global class, not bound by state (or taxation) that chooses to opt out – this new 'nationalism of wealth' is a threat to civilized society and we must understand it better if the constitution isn't to be blown up by a gunpowder plot of selfishness.

In this more considered process, we might ponder the basis of rights. My specialty is water resources. During the French Revolution, the flow of a river was equated with liberty. It is a nice image. It is also true, in that ready access to water determines the level of freedom for anyone. So too does land – if a person can't get land to grow crops, or build a house, or be free to roam, then they are not free. Liberty rests on resources, and is political at a secondary level.

You may not 'own' your land and water, but if an excessive charge is put on either, then your liberty is curtailed. If the resource is extracted, your chance of any quality of life may go with it. If richer folk come and dominate the resource, then you will be thrown off it. We don't think in these terms precisely because we have an abundance of both – though we are rightly irritated when feudal practices are used to justify huge land holdings.

How we deal with resources, ownership and the value of use (the rent) is the defining global issue of the 21st century, as it sits at the heart of food supply, climate change, sustainability and the survival of nations. Finding a constitution that could address this without severely affecting government and the healthy rivalry of ideas is a tough call.

Financial excess, climate change, disease and sustainability range across borders. Let us not write a constitution that feigns to be modern, but misses the truth.

If we step into this territory, we must do so with courage. It will not be good enough to repeat the phrases from other constitutions and UN statements, when history has taught us how easily such ideas are ignored or abused. Let's not write a document just to feel good.

On the flip side, lets not be unrealistic. If our liberties are determined by access to resources, then one of those is money. Of the spending we control, half of it goes on wages. Low wages must be raised to an equitable relationship with the highest. This may not be the stuff of 'rights' but it has a huge bearing on an individual's sense of worth.

Similarly it is a divine truth of politics that nobody threatens the NHS or pensions, but the Institute of Fiscal Studies warns that these two budgets will soon suck up most tax revenues. To what degree are the liberties of some curtailed by politicians too feart to challenge the assumptions of others? We need a sense of common purpose and shared values to deal fairly with the money we have, and the country we wish for our children.

There are many ways of making the debate real. Can you lose citizenship if you don't pay tax? Is neglect of child poverty a crime against humanity? Does a government's defense of spying on its citizens, and then trying to prosecute a war in Syria against the wishes of parliament, count as treason? All good fun for heated arguments across the country.

As for that opening paragraph of a constitution how about the following?

> I am restless for liberty, love and peace. I will not settle for so long as one hundred of us suffer poverty or injustice. It is my duty as a citizen of the world to contribute where I can and to respect the liberties of others. We are all passing by and none should be judged by race, gender, sex, religion, wealth or health, but by the quality of kindness, and judged in this world in the light of fairness and forgiveness.

You, dear reader, will do a better job. I am another member of the one per cent, passing through with the luck of a good education and a set of skills. The constitution should be informed by those who know injustice, poverty and discrimination – a mirror to us all. Then we should, regardless of class, have time to consider the truth of the words. And when the ink is dry, everyone should feel some loyalty to the meaning and the word, because it is nothing if we cannot act as a community, bound by the perfect tension between personal freedom and social justice. Yes, I like that.

Considering a constitution: A view from Iceland

THORVALDUR GYLFASON

In spite of clear popular support, Iceland's new crowd-sourced constitution was recently killed by politicians. An ex-member of the constitutional council sheds some light on what happened – and why there might still be some hope for this unique experiment.

Iceland earned the respect of many observers of democracy around the world when, after the financial crash of 2008, its parliament decided to go back to basics and revise the country's constitution. A constitutional overhaul was long overdue. For nearly 70 years, Iceland's political class had repeatedly promised and failed to revise the provisional constitution of 1944, which was drawn up in haste with minimal adjustment of the 1874 constitution as part of Iceland's declaration of independence from Nazi-occupied Denmark. Clearly, the 1944 constitution had not prevented the executive overreach and cronyism that paved the way for the corrupt privatization of the Icelandic banks from 1998 to 2003 – and their subsequent crash a few years later.

Faced by pots-and-pans banging crowds in Parliament Square in Reykjavík in late 2008 and early 2009, the politicians admitted failure, accepting the protesters' demands for, among other things, a new constitution.

The new post-crash government that came to office in early 2009 – the first majority government to include neither the centre-right Independence Party nor the agrarian Progressive Party – decided to break new ground by asking the people, not the politicians, to draft a new constitution. To this end, the parliament appointed a constitutional committee of seven to prepare the ground and organise a national assembly comprising 950 individuals drawn at random from the national registry.

The national assembly, organised in 2010 in accordance with the notion of Collective Intelligence,[1] concluded after a day's deliberations in Novem-

---

1 The 2010 assembly was modelled on a privately organised national assembly the year before.

ber that a new constitution was called for and ought to contain certain key provisions concerning, for example, electoral reform and the owner-ship of natural resources, for a long time two of the most contentious political issues in Iceland. In October of that year, the government also held a national election to a constituent assembly to which 25 individu-als were elected from a roster of 522 candidates from all walks of life, most of them with no particular political or special interest affiliations.

With the constituent assembly about to start its work in early 2011, some opposition politicians could not conceal their displeasure. The conclusion of the national assembly constituted an unequivocal appeal for the revocation of privileges – such as the privileges of those who benefit from unequal access to the country's common-property natural resources as well as from unequal voting rights. Understandably, the prospect of 25 individuals over whom the political parties had no control being about to begin their work guided by a legal mandate to revise the constitution in broad accord with the conclusions of the national assem-bly made some politicians uneasy.

What happened next? Three individuals with documented connections to the Independence Party, Iceland's largest political party until the crash of 2008, filed a bizarre technical complaint about the way the election to the constituent assembly had been conducted. On the basis of these comp-laints, six Supreme Court justices, five of whom had been appointed by successive ministers of justice from the Independence Party, declared the election null and void – even if no one had ever claimed that the results of the election were at all affected by the alleged technical flaws.

Never before had a national election in a fully-fledged democracy been invalidated on technical grounds. The parliament reacted to the ruling by appointing the 25 representatives who had received the most votes to a constitutional council, thereby changing a popularly elected assembly into one appointed by parliament. The opponents of constitu-tional change celebrated victory and thereafter used every opportunity to undermine the creditworthiness of the council.

The opposition was not confined to the Independence Party. The Progressives, who had previously expressed strong support for a new constitution, changed course and joined the opposition to reform. Even within the new governing coalition of the Social Democratic Alliance and the Left-Green Movement, there were pockets of passive resistance to change as well as among some academics apparently disappointed that *they* had not been asked to rewrite the constitution.

Whence the fierce opposition to constitutional reform? The chief opponents were the usual suspects: the political allies of special interest groups such as the fishing vessel owners whom the politicians had turned into a state within the state through *gratis*, or practically *gratis*, allocation of valuable fishing licenses. The opposition also came from politicians who would not stand much chance of being re-elected to parliament under the principle of 'one person, one vote' (as the current system requires many more votes to be elected as an MP in Reykjavik than in one of the more rural areas). Indeed, constitutionally protected national ownership of natural resources and electoral reform to ensure 'one person, one vote' were the two principal hallmarks of the bill.

But the constitutional council paid no attention to any of this. Within four months, it produced a constitutional bill incorporating virtually all the conclusions of the national assembly, and approved the bill unanimously by 25 votes to zero, with no abstentions, and delivered the bill to parliament in mid-2011. In the course of preparing the bill, the council sought and received the advice of numerous experts in different areas as well as from ordinary citizens who were invited to offer their comments and suggestions on the council's interactive website. Representatives of special interest groups, unused to not being invited to exclusive legislative meetings, did not respond to this open invitation to the public. After the bill was completed, they could not rightly complain that they had not been consulted.

After delivering the bill to parliament, the constitutional council disbanded. The parliament took over, seeking further comments from local lawyers as well as, ultimately, from the Venice Commission. The parliament was encouraged to translate the bill into English so as to be able to solicit foreign expert opinion, but failed to respond. Instead, a translation was arranged and paid for by the Constitutional Society, a private non-profit organization. This translation made it possible for world-renowned constitutional experts such as Prof. Jon Elster from Columbia University and Prof. Tom Ginsburg from the University of Chicago to express their helpful views of the bill.

The bill was brought to a national Referendum in late 2012. Initially, the parliament intended the Referendum to coincide with the presidential election in June 2012 to secure a good turnout, but the opposition Independence Party and Progressive Party resorted to filibuster to thwart this plan, holding parliament hostage for days and weeks on end.

At the same time, they complained about not having enough time to consider the bill – which was, of course, largely due to their reluctance to accept and follow the constitutional process. When the Independence Party leader was reminded of the classic example of *chutzpah* (this is when you murder your parents and ask for mercy on the grounds that you are an orphan), he complained about being unfairly likened to a murderer.

Nevertheless, the Referendum was delayed until October 2012. Voter turnout was 49 per cent. No less than 67 per cent of the electorate declared their support for the bill as well as for its key individual provisions such as national ownership of natural resources (83 per cent said Yes) and equal voting rights, meaning one person, one vote (67 per cent said Yes). By inviting the voters to accept or reject the bill *in toto* (specifically, the first question on the ballot was: 'Do you want the proposals of the Constitutional Council to form the basis of a legislative bill for a new Constitution?') as well as its key individual provisions, the parliamentary majority was able to say to the bill's opponents: Look, the voters support both the bill as a whole *and* its key provisions. In view of the results, parliament decided to suggest only changes of wording where considered necessary and to abstain from substantive changes (except concerning the church where the voters did not accept the formulation in the bill). The people had spoken.

The path forward, however, proved tricky. Three of the seven members of the constitutional committee which had been fairly unanimous in its work criticized the bill, unmoved by the result of the Referendum, conducting themselves *ex post* like agents of the parliamentary opposition to the bill. The majority of four is known to support the bill and to respect the result of the Referendum. A committee of lawyers asked by parliament to suggest only changes of wording went beyond its mandate by, among other things, suggesting substantive changes to the natural resource clause in a poorly disguised attempt to thwart the intent of the constitutional council and the will of the voters as expressed in the Referendum. The council had made it clear in its proposed constitutional provision as well as in its supporting documents that the allocation of fishing quotas does not bestow on the recipients of such allocations any private property rights to the common-property resources. To its credit, the parliamentary committee in charge restored the council's original formulation.

There was no dearth of academic viewpoints on the council as five of its 25 members were professors and three others were junior academics. But unlike the many academic experts who generously offered their help and advice to the council during its four months of intensive work in 2011, a few others were less forthcoming.

It was only after the October 2012 Referendum that some of the unsupportive academics stepped forward with critical comments on the bill, presented in newspaper articles and television interviews as well as at a series of conferences organized by some universities. The criticism offered was generally of low quality on top of being late, reflecting personal opinions rather than academic research as well as total disregard for the timetable laid down by parliament.

In a newspaper interview, after the Referendum, one professor called the council 'completely illegitimate,' adding that 'a certain elite' (presumably including himself) should rewrite the constitution. The poor timing of this late criticism is noteworthy because the Alliance for a New Constitution, a private association established to explain the constitutional bill to the voters before the Referendum, had written to the rectors of the universities ahead of the Referendum, asking them to encourage their experts to contribute to public debate on the bill. Their reaction appeared only after the Referendum. It seems that the dissenting academics hoped the bill would be rejected in the Referendum and thought it unnecessary to discuss it.

A month after the Referendum, parliament at last asked the Venice Commission for its reaction to the bill. In record time, Venice produced a draft report with various suggestions, several of which the relevant parliamentary committee decided to incorporate into the bill. The bill was now ready for a final vote in parliament. A majority of 32 MPs out of 63 declared in public and in writing that they supported the bill and wanted it passed before parliament was dissolved in time for the April election. Based on earlier related votes in parliament, it seemed likely that only 15 or 20 MPs would vote against the bill; the October 2012 Referendum was approved by 35 votes against 15, with 13 abstentions. Victory seemed assured.

But was it? The main opposition parties, the Independence Party and the Progressives, threatened a final act of filibuster, a tactic they had used successfully to delay the 2012 Referendum and to derail and destroy various other legislative initiatives of the government. (In a telling comparison, one pro-constitution MP likened her attempts to get work done in parliament to trying to file her income tax return with monkeys at the kitchen table.) The government majority behind the bill, including a small opposition party, the Movement, did have the legislative means to stop the filibuster to prevent time from running out but they were reluctant to do so, even if it was clear that failing to do so would kill the bill.

I received advance warnings from MPs that the bill would not be passed; 'I smell sulphur,' one MP wrote to me. Some council members with good connections to parliament had warned all along that parliamentary support for the bill was rather weak. The strategy of the Alliance for a New Constitution was to force the issue into the open. We understood from the outset that in a secret ballot the bill might fail in parliament; after all, rising against the fishing vessel owners in Iceland has been described as 'suicide' for rural MPs.

Parliament does not vote in secret, however, and this was key. In an attempt to ensure that the constitutional bill would have to be brought to a vote, Margrét Tryggvadóttir MP presented the bill put forward by the parliamentary committee in charge (of which she was a member) as an amendment to another related last-minute bill. But the president of the parliament put the last-minute bill to a vote without first presenting the amendment, thereby failing to bring the constitutional bill to a vote, in violation of parliamentary procedure. This happened at 2 a.m. on the morning of the last session of parliament before recess. The enemies of constitutional reform carried the day and democracy was put on ice. The government blamed the misbehaving opposition for the debacle, while the outgoing prime minister who had launched the process in 2009 said this was the saddest day of her 35 years in parliament.

The April 2013 election produced a coalition government of the Independence Party and the Progressives, the two parties that privatized the banks *à la Russe* and set the stage for the crash of 2008. The parties represented in parliament hardly mentioned the constitution in the campaign; they wanted to avoid the subject. The Progressives won the election by promising instant household debt relief. In office, the first thing they did – surprise, surprise – was to arrange instant tax relief for the fishing vessel owners. It is clear that the two parties have no intention of reviving the constitutional bill. To them, it does not matter that 67 per cent of the electorate expressed support for the bill and its key provisions. Further, they have decided to put Iceland's 2009 application for EU membership on ice. Expect more ice to come.

As always, however, there will be a new parliament after this one. One day, most probably, the constitutional bill approved by the people of Iceland in the 2012 Referendum or a similar one will become the law of the land. Stay tuned.

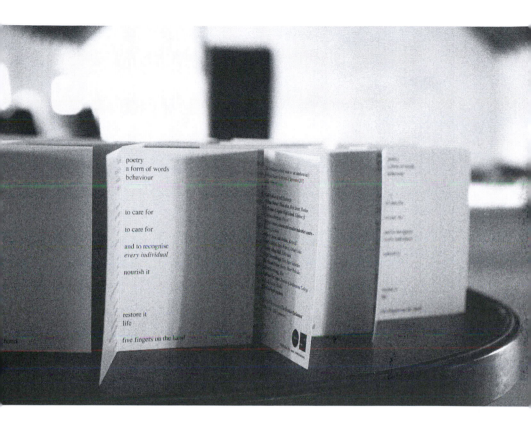

Considering a constitution: A view from the Red Paper Collective

PAULINE BRYAN

The Red Paper for Scotland was first published in 1975 with Gordon Brown as its Editor. It played a significant role in establishing the centrality of devolution in Labour Movement thinking. Thirty years later in 2005 a second Red Paper for Scotland was published, edited by Vince Mills. This volume explored the challenges facing Scotland, at that time, under a New Labour government in Westminster and six years after the establishment of the Scottish Parliament. A third Red Paper for Scotland was published in 2013[3] and will continue the tradition of exploring the challenges for socialists in Scotland and elsewhere in the lead up to the Referendum in 2014.

The debate on Scotland's future has focused on a range of constitutional options from full independence, as proposed by the SNP, to fiscal autonomy under Devolution Max and a modified status quo under the 2012 Scotland Act. Though apparently very different, all have one thing in common. They focus on structures. They do not ask what these powers are *for*. As Stephen Smellie put it to the 2012 STUC, 'the answer to all these questions is not a flag, a border or even a list of powers in Edinburgh and London. It is what you intend to do with these powers and for what purpose.'

In fact, these different constitutional proposals also have another feature in common – which is probably why they don't ask this question. All assume that the future Scotland, whatever its status, will operate within the same neo-liberal economic assumptions as apply at present. Markets will rule. A Scottish parliament, whatever its formal powers, would not seek to intervene to limit the free movement of capital or

---

3 The Red Paper on Scotland 2014, edited by Pauline Bryan and Tommy Kane, Glasgow Caledonian University Archives, 2013

commodities or to take significant ownership of productive resources. The current balance of power between capital and labour would remain.

The Red Paper Collective has entered the debate in order to put a quite different perspective. Its objective is to return the discussion on Scotland's future to the terms originally posed by the pioneers of the Scottish Labour movement when they argued for Home Rule in the 1920s or when the Scottish Trades Union Congress took up the demand for a Scottish Parliament in the 1970s. Then the purpose of a home rule parliament was seen quite clearly in terms of powers *for*. It would help shift the balance of power in favour of working people and it would do so by advancing *economic* democracy. Such a parliament would give elected representatives in Scotland the power enhance services, reduce social insecurity and promote the common ownership of utilities and productive sources – and in strengthening the position of working people in Scotland also strengthening the bargaining power of working people across Britain. Constitutional change was seen to be about linking democracy at national, Scottish level to class power at British level. It was about changing the balance.

Today this, if anything, has become even more important. We face an unprecedented economic crisis. It results directly from the imposition of neo-liberal, free market policies in face of the global dominance of the big financial institutions. The origins of this crisis can be traced back to the long-term withdrawal of the state from the economy and the deregulation of markets – resulting in the share of income going to employees falling, a massive expansion of credit to maintain purchasing power and then speculation in debt by the banks. The financial crisis, which broke out in 2008, was then turned into a long-term economic crisis by the application of the same neo-liberal policies. Governments raced to cut debt, slashed public expenditure and further reduced the share of income going to labour. The prospects for working people are worse than they have been at any time since 1945. The Welfare State is now directly under attack. This is why the demand for economic democracy is as relevant now as it was in previous crises in the 1930s and the 1970s – and why it is essential to take it into the debate on Scotland's future.

It is also critical for human rights. The need to address the issue of human rights was explicitly flagged up in the Scotland Act of 1998. This was reinforced by the Westminster parliament's 1998 Human Rights Act which required the legal incorporation of judgments arising from the European Court of Human Rights (ECHR). Scotland's Human Rights Commission was established in 2008 under the terms of the Scottish Commission for Human Rights Act passed in 2006.

The legal terms specifying human rights are important. The ECHR was established under the European Convention on Human Rights in 1950 at the initiative of the Council of Europe, a body which at that time also included the socialist states of Eastern Europe. Its terms are somewhat more comprehensive than those subsequently specified in the European Union's Charter of Fundamental Rights. On employment, for instance, the Convention specifies 'the right to work'. The EU's Charter simply ratifies 'the right to seek work'. Yet today, although all European countries are signatories to the Convention and the ECHR, there are over 20 million people without work in Europe. Legal rights by themselves are not enough.

This applies no less to Scotland. Its Human Rights Commission has made some progress on issues of gender equality and sexualities. It has also investigated the violation of the human rights of older people in care homes. At the same time cuts in budgets by the Scottish and Westminster parliaments have eroded rights to good education, social care, housing, libraries and transport. Some can afford them. Others increasingly cannot. Yet these are also essential rights.

This is why the Red Paper Collective stresses the importance of three things: specifying what the powers are *for*; matching them with the economic means to realise them; and, third and not least, linking such formal legal powers to an understanding that in a class society, where the resources are controlled by a minute minority, democracy must be used to mobilise the countervailing class power of the great majority. This is necessary for the work of any effective Scottish parliament. It must also be the case across Britain – because, as those who demanded Home Rule in the 1920s and 1970s knew only too well, the economic power of the owners of property, whether in Scotland or England and Wales, is vested in state institutions at British level.

This is why the Red Paper advocates a form of federalism. This not in the naïve belief that constitutions themselves, any more than formal declarations of human rights, can resolve basic issues of class power but in the knowledge that some constitutional arrangements can help and others can hinder. We need a mechanism that does not turn the UK into four neo-liberal economies vying with each other to be the lowest taxed and the lowest paid. We need to turn the diversity into a means of strengthening the power of working people.

The STUC, founded in 1897, first formally adopted a policy of support for a Scottish Parliament in 1914. The Independent Labour Party from its inception in 1893 had a commitment to Home Rule and played a prominent role within the Scottish Home Rule Association. Their demands were for a federal arrangement rather than for independence. The model of Home Rule for Scotland used by the STUC and Labour Party in Scotland included the devolution of power to deal with all issues except for foreign policy, customs and the crown. It would have seen a reduction in the number of Westminster MPs and importantly, the ability to redistribute wealth within the United Kingdom.

When George Buchanan moved the Scottish Home Rule Bill, introduced in 1924, the then Labour Government gave the general principle of the Bill its approval, but failed to allow time for its progress through the Commons.

In moving the Bill ILP member George Buchanan drew attention to the minutia of Scottish issues that had to be dealt with in the House of Commons, and how he as a Scottish MP was able to vote on matters such as the London Traffic Bill. He stated 'The English Members can rid themselves of Scottish representation as soon as they care to, for in our Bill we make this proposal, that whenever there is a scheme of devolution agreed on, to apply to England, Scotland and Wales, the Scottish Members will cease to take any part or interest in the affairs in which the English Parliament ought to take part.'

The Labour Movement's position, unlike the nationalist one, acknowledged the bonds the British working class had forged in two centuries of political struggle and recognised shared class interests over and above the shared interest of living in Scotland. Far from wanting to separate from the English they wanted to join with working people across the Islands in creating a socialist alternative. While campaigning for the devolution of powers the early pioneers adopted internationalism as their ideal, but wanted devolution of powers to create democratic federalism.

The STUC continued its support for Home Rule and then for Devolution, even though many of its affiliated Unions operated across Britain and some into Ireland. A delegate from the Scottish Miners (which supported Home Rule) demanding a UK Wages Board at the 1921 Congress stated that 'socialism, like capitalism, should know no boundaries and should look to the day when workers of all countries would become one great industrial organisation.' From the turn of the 20th Century onwards, the Labour Movement's demands for a Scottish Parliament were to enable it to tackle poverty, poor housing, inadequate public services and industrial closures and not for its own sake.

Now that we have the Scottish Parliament, Welsh and Northern Irish Assemblies we have the basis for a federal arrangement with power devolved but with the strength of a single Parliament dealing with macro economic issues and international relations. This dual approach will allow variations in policy within the constituent parts, but retain the combined strength to operate within the global economy.

What might a democratic federalist arrangement mean for Scotland? For a start it would resolve the West Lothian question. Scottish representatives would have the right to vote on issues that impacted on Britain as a whole and on Scotland in particular. They would not have the right to vote on issues that relate only to England or other parts of Britain. It would however safeguard the ability to redistribute wealth within the UK and allow the labour movements in the whole of Britain to collaborate in resisting attacks on working people. It would lessen the likelihood of a race to the bottom in making Scotland a low pay, low corporation tax economy. It would reduce the extent of the London-centric nature of the

Westminster Parliament which is as damaging to Lancashire as it is to Lanarkshire.

Dave Watson has outlined a model of fiscal devolution which, unlike Devo Max and Devo Plus, allows for a progressive approach to taxation. This would give a Scottish Government powers to redistribute wealth within Scotland, but also allow for redistribution across Britain. The power held by the Scottish Parliament could be used more flexibly to create a fairer tax system both nationally and locally that can improve public services and the pay and conditions of public employees and make requirements on private sector employers to pay a living wage.

We should support the extension of the capacity to borrow for capital and revenue purposes that go well beyond the limits set out in the Scotland Act. This should be used to end the Scottish Parliament's dependence on PPP, PFI and the Non-profit Distributing Projects of the present Scottish Government.

A Scottish Parliament should in appropriate situations, have the right to take land and enterprises into public control. These rights could be used to safeguard jobs and industries or where the best interests of those dependent on the land or the enterprise are in jeopardy.

A Scottish Government should be able to create publicly owned enterprises to rebuild Scotland's industrial base on green technology, renewable and high value manufacturing; addressing unemployment black spots and creating a more prosperous future for the people, especially the young people, of Scotland.

What we acknowledge is that since the establishment of the Scottish Parliament and greater powers going to the Welsh Assembly there will inevitably be change at Westminster. The Tories are dodging the West Lothian Question, but it will not go away. Carwyn Jones, leader of the Welsh Assembly, has called for a Constitutional Convention for the UK. He states, '... for me, devolution is not about how each of Wales, Scotland and Northern Ireland are separately governed. Rather it is about how the UK is governed, not by one but by four administrations, and which are not in a hierarchical relationship one to another.' He also states 'representatives of all the states should come together and agree amongst themselves what limited range of powers should be conferred "upwards" on the federal authority.'

Both the STUC and the Scottish Labour Party are establishing commissions to consider the case for greater powers for the Scottish Parliament. Both organisations state that the criterion used to support a position will be whether it is in the best interests of the people of Scotland.

The role of the Red Paper Collective is to influence the debates within the labour and trade union movement and to ensure that Scotland's progressive and democratic traditions of working class struggle become the driving for change – and in doing so ensure that human rights exist not just on paper but in reality.

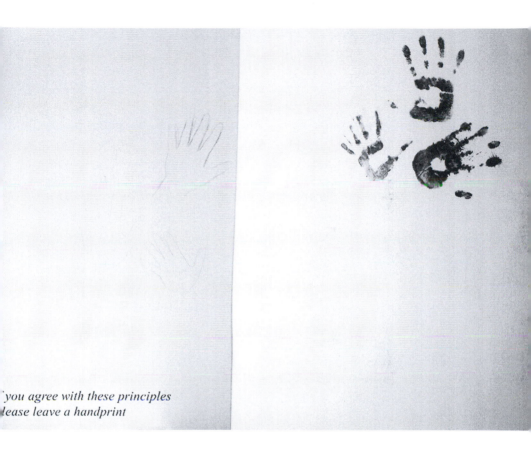

you agree with these principles
lease leave a handprint

Considering a constitution: A view across the Meadows

DANNY ZINKUS

I was asked to imagine living in a country that had a simple and powerful statement of our shared values written into our constitution, and I've had Call for a Constitution up on the sitting room window of my flat in Marchmont for a few weeks now. What if we lived in a country where every citizen had learnt the principles expressed in the poem in school? What if everyone could carry around in their back pocket a statement of our shared values, like a red card to be brandished when someone broke the social contract?

I think a shared statement of these values that was strongly felt in our culture would require us to be a democracy where power flowed up from people and local communities. At the moment power in our political system is concentrated. Influence lies with a narrow type of person; it does not sit with us. Every few years or so we are asked to choose between one group of pretty much identical politicians or another who will behave in more or less the same way. Those who wield power in our country do not have to ask our opinion, so they do not. Power flows out and downward from the centre.

If we had a strong statement of values, such as these words, front and centre in our constitution and woven into every part of it, it would give individuals and communities power. At best we would have the right to be involved in decisions that affect us. The right to be an active part of our own political community. A positive ability to work with others to shape our own lives. We would have a country woven through with a commitment to the human element in all decision-making. A country where we see people not as objects or the mere means to the ends of the rich and powerful but as vibrant and valuable selves. At worst we would be armed with power to say no: the power to force everybody else to the negotiating table and to need to make a collective decision that represented the interest of everyone involved. A negative, blocking power, but a power we lack as things stand.

How does such a simple statement of value give us so much power? It starts and ends with the notion that such values are powerfully resonant in our lives and communities so that everyone can immediately see when they are being promoted and when they are being treated with disdain. It starts with these values living in the words and deeds of every person in the country, but it requires such values to guide the making of our laws and policies. The principles must inform how laws and policies are applied.

Why these values and not others? As they stand, this is a powerful expression, simply stated and memorable, of a social contract that embodies tolerance, mutual responsibility and universal empowerment: it gives the poorest and weakest the power to say no to the richest and strongest in the knowledge that the power to do so is backed up by universal consent.

* * *

To have the words on the window feels as though the words of a conversation have fixed themselves to the window, and fixed as they are they are having an aesthetic effect on my home, and a social effect as my home spills out onto the street, and the street spills in through the window. They look stunning up there, and you can't help but notice people's eyes being drawn to them as they pass by.

The words are hard to read from inside the house. They are backwards, mirror-writing, and cast themselves as a shadow on the far wall of the sitting room. They fade in and out as the sun shines brightly, or slops behind a cloud, like a conversation being half listened to. They move at the pace of the sun's progress across the deep red of the wall. When I sit there and see the words appear, I'm aware that the light and shadow must be hanging in the middle of the room, invisible except for where it meets a solid surface. The effect is very beautiful.

So, we have words that spill out from the room into the street, and reflect back from the street into the room. The effect is to break down the

division between public and private. To expose the connection between the social and the political. If we want these values to shape the contents of our laws and lives, then they must be visible and accessible to us on a day-to-day basis. We need people to be able to say clearly what our national values are. We need any individual to be able to see clearly when the spirit of our constitution has been broken. We need individuals and communities to expect to be engaged in any decision-making process, and to be able to participate directly in decisions that affect their livelihoods.

I think that the flow of norms runs from these five values to a discussion of our rights and duties in detail, to a series of statements of national intent and then into the day-today detail of law and policy and executive action. Where there is a conflict between our fundamental values and executive action then each individual should have the power to say 'Stop, that is unconstitutional' and to trigger a review by a powerful constitutional court, and an appeal in court should trump the legislation. The court needs to sit as part of the community and its power should flow from the consent and understanding of the people. Its remedy is to say to the powerful: 'Go back and do a fairer deal!' And so, just as the US constitution and the European Charter of Human Rights can be invoked to strike down legislation or policy decision, so the detailed rights and obligations that arise from a strong statement of nationally shared values must have *direct effect* for it to be a tool in the hands of the ordinary citizen, gaining him and her a place at the negotiating table when legislation is discussed.

* * *

The most striking thing about the half-public, half-private nature of the words is how surreptitious people are about looking at it when they think I am around. I've seen people pause as they walk past to read it, then seeing me seeing them scurry on as if they'd broken stride and hadn't really been looking at anything. If we enter or leave the flat whilst someone is reading the poem, they will dash off as if they'd been caught intruding into a private thing. On my way home I've become practised at spotting people reading the poem and pretending that I'm just walking past to give them the time to finish reading it. I think I'm trying to create a private space in public for them to enter, in public, into the private space of their thoughts and my window.

* * *

What words do we want to live by?

The best place to start is with a strong and simple statement of fundamental values that all citizens can recall and carry with them. We ask ourselves: what do we mean, in practice, by these words. We deliberate and agree what these values require and then create a statement of aims for our nation that lays out in detail how the state should meet the needs of our citizens. And we do all this again in twenty years time, respecting the ability of the citizen of the future to manage their affairs as much as we respect the citizen of today.

This means more than people getting involved in partisan politics: it means that people are ready and willing to lead citizen initiatives and petitions, to serve on court and citizen juries and in citizen assemblies. The flip side of citizens taking part is that officials should respect peoples' right to take part, to actively seek their views, and to consider themselves bound by the outcomes of the consultations they run.

Here is the red card in action. Imagine a piece of ill-conceived legislation based on a flawed consultation. It has not respected the communities it affects. It is out of order and struck down. Faced with powerful individual and community rights it would be so much easier to do the consultation process properly in the first place.

For our democracy to be more *participative*, the power must flow up from individuals to local communities, to regional communities to national assemblies. The most potent way of holding power locally is to raise and spend taxes locally: local control over public money ensures that local voices are heard when decisions are made.

For our democracy to be more *deliberative* requires a model in which people are equal, and consensus is the goal. Using tools like citizen juries and citizen assemblies, a deliberative democracy takes ordinary people at random and gives them the power of information and the luxury of time. One of the core strengths of deliberative democracy is its ability to link practical politics to the deeper question of who we are. A constitution with strongly held rights would encourage this. Strong constitutional rights are not just protection from an over-mighty state, nor a set of requirements to be delivered by a bureaucracy. Strong constitutional rights are a demand that we too become involved in delivering and safeguarding what we value.

And this is reflected in the law. The law as written down is only a prediction about what a court will do. The law is not an apolitical technical process. The school of jurisprudence called American Legal Realism sees the judicial process as being deeply rooted in the values of judges and jurors. Judges and jurors make their decisions based not only on the written law but also on the values they hold in common. And where there is a clear popular understanding of our shared values then individuals can see where the judicial process has stood up for our values, or ignored them. To be able to hold judges and jurors to account is a potent tool for protecting and promoting our values.

* * *

Which brings me to the process of getting the poem up in my house, which was not as straightforward as early conversations with Angus had lead either of us to believe. This window isn't the window in an art gallery of a public museum: it is also the window of my wife's sitting room in her private house.

So the process of installing the poem in the window was a process of negotiation and compromise. A process where the lofty ideals of a public work of art clashed with mundane considerations about the cost of repainting the wall. Where the intellectual experiment of inviting people to engage in a discussion of shared values runs hard up against the faces of strangers pushed up against the glass to see what else you have in your home.

The process of negotiating with my wife about when the poem could go up and for how long, and whether we would incorporate a 'response wall' was a microcosmic version of the process of incorporating ideals into the fabric of our national life that had to meet the values that are real and potent in our everyday lives. It didn't lead to marital tension, but it was something that required working through with respect for different points of view. It meant that the poem is there, but for a defined period of time, an answer that met everyone's needs.

The poem talks about different obligations, different elements in the way people can live together as fellow and full human beings. I think that the process of putting the poem up has been a small but important exploration of how living with real and potent values in your life is hard but rewarding work.

onstitutio
everyone to respect and
communities
and
to care for *the land*
and wherever
the land has been abused to
restore it
so that it can support
all forms of
life
nourish i
and to re
to care f

Epilogue: The White Paper

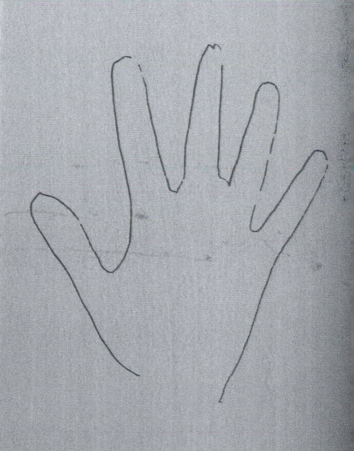

know your
values!

Bruce Crawford
MSP

CHAPTER FIVE

Epilogue: The White Paper

OK – SO LET'S EXAMINE what the white paper says about the constitution. First of all, amid all the positive talk about what a constitution is: 'a statement of intent for the nation' and 'the basis of everyday life' that 'defines who makes decisions and how the people choose those decision makers' there is a clear fudge. A constitution, as has been shown elsewhere in this book, is 'not the act of a government, but that of a people constituting a government'. Those words of Tom Paine run like a knife through the rhetoric of the White Paper. It never dares to imagine that a government should be not just elected, but *constituted* by the people. This is the paradox at the heart of the White Paper: on the one hand it states what it terms to be 'the fundamental constitutional truth, that the people, rather than politicians or state institutions are the sovereign authority in Scotland' and yet on the other it gives no opportunity for the people to exercise any power, or even to express themselves except on highly restricted terms and according to a schedule that the government has decided. This schedule postpones the authority of the people for at least three years, and probably forever. It is not good enough.

So, how does an authoritarian agenda, aimed at fortifying the power of the parliamentary elite and the party system disguise itself behind populist rhetoric?

Point 529 asks what 'sovereignty of the people' means and answers that 'the people of Scotland have the right to choose freely their form of governance'. Not just which MSPs will represent them, but the whole 'form of governance'. So – let's make that choice if it is our fundamental right! However, in the opinion of the White Paper, a right only becomes fundamental when the government say it is. In the present it counts for nothing, and only applies to the distant future. The right to choose is forbidden by this document, and explicitly in these words:

... the right time for a written constitution is after independence, not before.[1]

Says who? Says those who don't want any pesky 'people' interfering with their power. Does a fundamental right only become such after the SNP have achieved their aim? How fundamental is it at all? The reality is that we need a constitution to bind those who take decisions in our name whatever the outcome of the Referendum, and this delaying tactic, explicitly endorsed by the White Paper in order to force a particular outcome, is an anti-democratic and authoritarian move, and deeply worrying. When I asked Nicola Sturgeon[2] – who is the minister responsible – why the Scottish Government had made no move towards a constitution she replied that it was 'outwith the government's legal competence'. This book challenges that assumption as it must be challenged throughout the UK: how can the contract by which we allow politicians to exercise power on our behalf ever be outside the legal competence of those doing it? This is a formula intended to keep people at arms length from the political process. The plan, as outlined, demonstrates their reluctance to engage at all with any agenda that stands for the empowerment of people and the binding of a parliament. This plan is the blueprint for a single-chamber parliamentary dictatorship, a constitutional arrangement that is even worse than Westminster. Ask yourself when you choose which way to vote in the Referendum: do we trust the government to such an extent that we would willingly give them absolute power? The constitution is in a similar position to the promise made at the White Paper's launch, of universal child-care: if it is a good thing and would make for a fairer society, then why not have it now? The purpose of this book is to call for that constitution now, and to call for parliamentarians to debate it now. Equally, the time to talk about a constitution in the whole of the UK is now, and it has been like that since 1647.

---

1 *Scotland's Future: from the Referendum to Independence and a written constitution*, p. 561.
2 At an exceedingly well attended public meeting on the 6 March 2014, at Broughton High School, Edinburgh

Let's look at the model proposed for making a constitution after 'independence'. Can it be trusted? There wont even be a start until two years after the Referendum, in 2016, when the White Paper proposes that a 'constitutional convention' is established. Who is involved in that? 'Everyone' asserts the white paper. How? According, says the White Paper, to the Icelandic 'crowd-sourced constitution' model. This is in the teeth of the fact that the Icelandic constitution has been and continues to be blocked by an all-powerful parliament, in hoc to narrow interests as Professor Gylfason has outlined in his essay for this book. That experiment has been tried once, and has failed, first compromised and then defeated by parliament; so why is it being proposed by the Scottish Government? Assuming that the government are aware of the truth of the Icelandic experiment, which is fair to say, this can only be interpreted as a hypocritical gesture: the pretence of making a constitution to bind a parliament in the knowledge that the parliament will get its way and that the peoples' voice is irrelevant. Their schedule puts any popular sovereignty so far in the distant future that there is no need to discuss it: we wouldn't find out whether we have any sovereignty or influence until 2017, three years hence, at the very earliest. Notice too who is in the driving seat when it comes to making this constitution law: '… it is for the Constitutional Convention (appointed by the government) to consider and for the Scottish Parliament to decide'. The people – those who 'have the right to choose freely their form of governance' turn out to have no say whatsoever. This is laughable, and characteristic of a policy document that pretends to represent people but that concedes no power whatsoever to them. It is a classic government fudge, and is a strategy to assure the indefinite postponement of popular sovereignty.

And remember, in the meantime, for at least three years by their own timetable, possibly more and most likely forever, the White Paper has delivered us an all-powerful parliament that has absolutely no brake on its power, no accountability outside elections, no second chamber and no constitution to bind its behaviour and its absolute power. The SNP plan is succinctly summed up in the paper that Nicola Sturgeon published ahead of the White Paper: it aims to 'complete the powers of the Parliament',[3] not to empower the Scottish people. It would be worst possible start for any new country, and is a recipe for democratic disaster.

The way to make popular sovereignty work would be to give people power from the start. The reason that many Parent Councils work so well as a way of involving parents in the running of schools in Scotland is that, from the very beginning, they were given the power to appoint head teachers. Give people the power, and they step up to the job. But the paper has nothing to say on the issue of the empowerment of people. It is, however explicitly clear about the amount of power that that government and the parliament should have. In particular it is greedy for 'all the powers of Westminster':

> On independence... the Scottish Parliament will control all areas of policy that are currently reserved to the Westminster...

This is a typical sentence from the White Paper, and characteristic of its eagerness to assert a wholesale assumption of powers for the Scottish Parliament. There are countless examples of this kind of sentence throughout the book. But please: note that misprint '*the* Westminster'. Something has been half changed here. It should read, not 'the Westminster' but 'the UK parliament' because that is what it is. Were it fair, it would balance either 'the Scottish Parliament' with 'the UK Parliament', or 'Holyrood' with 'Westminster'. But – as is characteristic of the SNP tendency to coercive discourse and of this document in particular – it uses rhetoric to mask reality. The Scottish Parliament sounds important and inclusive, but the UK Parliament is downplayed to what must have been 'the Westminster Parliament'. Then the word parliament was removed as it suits the rhetoric to deny any democratic credentials to Westminster/the UK parliament. The UK parliament cannot be admitted to include MPs that represent and act in the interest of Scotland. So, the ideological proofreader, wanting to weight the sentence to suggest that Scotland equals democracy and Westminster equals tyranny, removes the word parliament

---

3 *Scotland's Future: from the Referendum to Independence and a written constitution*, para 1:1; February 2013.

and in the half-million pound rush to produce the document leaves the typo. If the 'the' had not been there if would still have been an unfair way to balance the two governments, but the typo indicates haste, and shows that there is a conscious manipulation going on. This may seem like a quibble over a typing error, but that sentence is important, and it sums up what the White Paper is all about: the assertion of the right of the parliamentary class to seize enormous and unchecked power. And the error allows us to see through to the anxiety and brinksmanship that attends this assertion, contrary to the smooth and reassuring tone that the book strives to achieve. The White Paper is not just made from a coercive rhetoric, it is made from a hasty, anxious rhetoric. If you wish to see it for yourself you can view it in any of the 20,000 copies of the first edition of the book, on page 362, Part 4, Chapter 10 'Building a Modern Democracy'. You can also view it in the same place online.

So, according to the paper, the Scottish Parliament will control all areas of policy currently reserved to *the* Westminster, and to give none of the civil rights, which citizens in the UK do not have without a constitution. The White Paper is clear that it approves of the UK model:

> ... we intend that the rights and responsibilities which accompany Scottish citizenship will be broadly in line with those currently aligned with British citizenship... with independence sovereignty would be formally invested in the people of Scotland...[4]

In other words, the sovereignty of the people is a fine phrase, but meaningless to the makers of this document in terms of giving power to people. Another tell-tale word is 'formally'. Why 'formally'? Why not 'genuinely'? This is because the government intends to be a copy of Westminster, minus the Lords and the tradition of 'precedents' that has stood in as an ad-hoc defender of peoples' rights, and the plan is to postpone any active and effective constitutional change that does any more than to pay lip-service to people's powers and peoples' rights. Even the most

---

4 *Scotland's Future: from the Referendum to Independence and a written constitution*, p. 495.

extreme neo-liberal austerity mongers can only dream of that kind of untrammelled parliamentary power.

We must pay attention to the way that the word 'people' is used in this document, as the transfer of power is, as foreseen in the White Paper, always to the government, and never to people. When it states 'Scotland' it does not mean the people of Scotland, but the ruling elite of Scotland. In our name, and with no concession to our desire to choose, the government takes all.

We must also pay attention to the language of lame double-think that is being used in this document. For example, it is, they say their plan to '... extend the powers of the Scottish Parliament and Scottish Government into all policy areas whilst retaining the separation of powers between executive and legislature...' It sounds fine, doesn't it, that we will have a kosher separation of powers like the Americans. But how will they achieve this? The executive (the government) is totally embedded in the legislative (the parliament) and members of the government are sitting MSPs. Are they implying that they intend to change this arrangement? Or, are they paying lip-service to the sixth year modern studies curriculum, without thinking through the implications of their own words? This kind of intellectual laziness is something that the newly enfranchised 16 and 17 year olds would do well to examine closely in the classroom.

And let us look at another categorical power grab by parliamentarians that is made explicitly in this document:

Will the Scottish Parliament have a second chamber? No.[5]

Here is clarity from the SNP on one simple issue. There will be nothing to hold back a majority decision at Holyrood, no peoples' assembly, and no Lords. This is not to say that the House of Lords is acceptable when we don't vote for it, and a Peoples' Chamber would be a far better alternative, but at least the House of Lords can scrutinise and delay legislation. This essential role is explicitly denied by the White Paper: '... the

---

5 *Scotland's Future: from the Referendum to Independence and a written constitution*, p. 572.

House of Lords will no longer be involved in legislating for Scotland...'.
If Alex Salmond wants to continue to ignore the rights for example of
Mike Forbes and to big up Donald Trump, or to do backdoor deals with
Jim Ratcliffe over the treatment of the workforce at Grangemouth and
the development of that plant for the profit of INEOS shareholders, then
there is nothing to check that exercise of power.

Remember, it was Alex Salmond who personally offered all the help
he could to assist Fred Goodwin and RBS in the disastrous takeover of the
Dutch bank, ABN Amro in 2007[6] which was the catastrophe that ruined
RBS. If Scotland has a moment akin to the 'Darien' disaster of 1700, a
moment when the government made a financial speculation that ruined
the country and compromised its independence, then that was it. Are we
prepared to hand over absolute and unchecked power to such a party,
given their closeness to the leaders of banks and business, and the record
of such flawed judgement?

This is positively dangerous: it is the grounds for an SNP coup d'etat.
They call it 'one chance in a generation', and it is their chance, once in a
generation, for a total power grab. No! No to that! No to the Yes-men!

However there are other voices in the Scottish Parliament, notably
that of Joanne Lamont, that is at least a rhetoric unlike that of the White
Paper: a rhetoric that is committed to the empowerment of people. We
think that our modest proposal can challenge her, the Labour party and
any sincere democrat in Scottish political life to bring that debate forward,
and to win. It would make for an irreversible first step in the right direction, it only takes one MSP to introduce a debate.

The White Paper has one other astonishing assertion about the future
constitution. It asks 'Do we need to know all this?' It may well be that
members of the government have no experience of or interest in what a
constitution can do and think that the public share their ignorance.
However, that is not the case in society at large. While I'm not a Rangers

---

6 See *The Herald Scotland*, 8/8/2010, Tom Gordon: 'Revealed: Salmond's support
for Goodwin over disastrous RBS deal'.

supporter, the example of the difficulties at Rangers Football Club is instructive. Because of bad financial practise, the club went into administration. This is the response of the Rangers' board as they attempt to appoint an honest chairman, as reported by *The Glasgow Herald*:

'Rangers Constitution' to be published

Richard Wilson
Sports writer
Saturday 30 November 2013

The nominees seeking election as Rangers directors at the forthcoming annual meeting will publish a written Rangers Constitution next week.

Paul Murray, Malcolm Murray, Alex Wilson and Scott Murdoch – want the document to be signed by all future directors and act as a binding commitment to certain values and pledges to ensure the long-term well-being of the club.

Rangers are at least clear about the order of events that is going to help the club: first you write the constitution, and then you invite the new directors to sign it. If they don't sign it they don't get the job, and if they break it they are fired. If Rangers can see the value of a constitution and can propose one quickly and practically, then why can the government and the Parliament not do the same? The value of a constitution is clearly understood across many institutions in Scotland, and used not as an afterthought, but well in advance, as a way to ensure 'a binding commitment to certain values and pledges to ensure long-term well-being'. That is common sense, and applies to Scotland and the UK as a whole: first we write the constitution, and then we appoint the government to act in our interests. If Rangers management know the value of a constitution as the first step, then how come the government of Scotland is so blind to it, and so shy of it? The club does things in that order to in order to avoid a power-grab from future directors, and to avoid behaviour that is self-interested, cynical and opportunist. Good luck to them, and it had better be a good constitution. And at the very least we need the same safe-guard not just for the Scottish government, but for that of the whole UK. In Scotland the debate is open in a way it has not been for a long time, and more open than anywhere else in the UK, and we have the chance to lead by example.

And remember: parliaments, with their control of power and patronage, do not readily concede power to those they purport to represent. If the history of the UK is a guide, it is only in special circumstances that such progressive steps are made: when the government is *on the back foot*. In Scotland, we have a government committed to a referendum that every poll suggests it is likely to lose, and these are just such circumstances.

This book cannot advocate support of the government's coercive power fantasies, and it does not support the status quo. More powers to the Scottish government? No! More powers to Scottish people! And especially, more powers to Scottish women! We want to see the government of Scotland become an institution that it has so far failed to be: an institution committed to the sovereignty of the people, to peoples' rights and powers and to their authority to choose how they wish to be governed. This is an on-going struggle, and the Referendum perhaps gives Scots the chance to do something far more ambitious than independence: a one in a generation chance to make a constituted government and to lead the rest of the UK by example. That is the prize.

In a federated uk, in which the people of its constituent parts have power over the decisions that affect them, a constituted government in Scotland is the first step. And we propose a way to start: to debate the five principles in full session of parliament – and they have the advantage of being 140 syllables, rather than 650 pages – to endorse them and then to give them to the people of Scotland decide. Then, at least there is a chance for one part of the UK to have the opportunity to experience what it is like to have words by which to hold their government to account.

And astonishingly, given our rich political history, for *the first time ever* in the history of these isles.

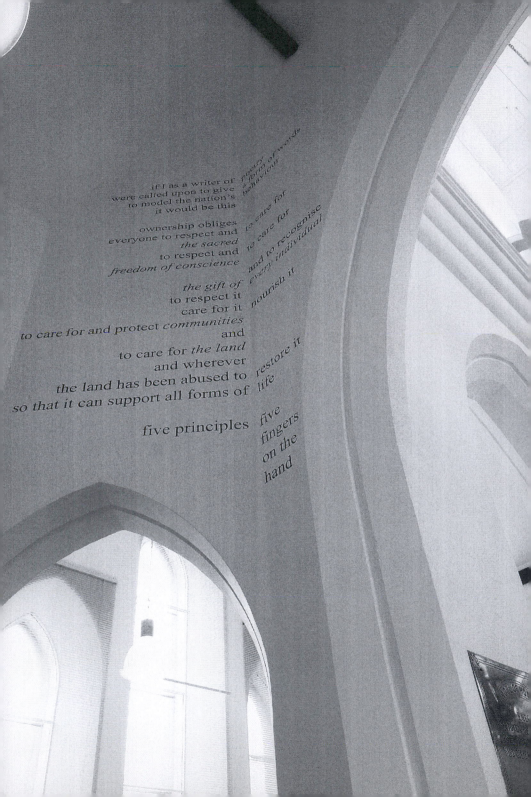

if I as a writer of *poetry*
a form of words
were called upon to give
behaviour
to model the nation's
it would be this

ownership obliges
to care for
everyone to respect and
the sacred
to care for
to respect and
freedom of conscience
and to recognise
every individual

the gift of
to respect it
nourish it
care for it
to care for and protect *communities*
and
to care for *the land*
and wherever
the land has been abused to *restore it*
so that it can support all forms of *life*

five principles *five*
fingers
on the
hand

Let this be
the philosophy
for a new
generation.

Acknowledgements

Many thanks to Sheila and Mike Forbes,

to Kenny MacAskill MSP for sponsoring the showing in the Scottish Parliament

to Gavin, Lydia and Louise at Luath Press,

to Crawfy and Katy at cca signs for many last minute vinyls,

to Russell McGovern for the Mill of Menie photos,

to Gavin Lockhart for the Skerray photos,

to Karen Fraser for the Shetland Library photos,

to Christine Gunn for the Thurso photos,

and to the TUC Library Collection at London Metropolitan University.

All other images by Angus Reid.

Contributors

GARY AMOS is Library and Archive manager at the Orkney Library and Archive, Kirkwall.

DONALD ANDERSON is Literature Development Officer for Shetland Arts.

PHIL ARCHER has been Principal of Leith School of Art, Edinburgh, since 1991.

ALEX BELL is a former BBC correspondent and also formerly head of policy and speechwriter to Alex Salmond. He is the author of *Peak Water*, and co-founder of allmediascotland.com.

PAULINE BRYAN is a member of and regular contributor to the Red Paper Collective, and a spokesperson for the Scottish Labour Campaign for Socialism. She regularly chairs meetings at the STUC.

MARY DAVIS is a Visiting Professor at Royal Holloway, University of London and was formerly Professor of Labour History at London Metropolitan University. She has written, broadcast and lectured widely on women's history, labour history, imperialism and racism. Her published books include *Comrade or Brother? A history of the British Labour Movement 1789–1951* (2009); Marxism & Struggle (1998); *Fashioning a New World: A history of the Woodcraft Folk* (2000); *Sylvia Pankhurst: a life in Radical Politics* (1999) and *Class and Gender in British Labour History* (2011). She was recipient of the TUC Woman's Gold Badge in 2010.

CHRISTINE DE LUCA is one of the foremost contemporary poets in Scotland. Born and brought up in Shetland, she has published five collections of poetry in English and Shetlandic. The first two of these won the Shetland Literary Prize, and a bilingual selected poems, Mondes Parallèles, (éditions fédérop, 2007) won the poetry Prix du Livre Insulaire.

COLIN DONATI was brought up Galloway, the Borders, Ayrshire and Moray, and now lives in Leith. A poet, translator and musician, he writes in both Scots and English. His work has been widely published in magazines, and his collections are Rock is Water, or a History of the Theories of Rain (Kettillonia, 2002) and Ancient and Now (Red Squirrel, 2010).

JANA EMBUREY is a professional artist. Originally from Slovakia, Jana has lived in Scotland for over 13 years. She has lived for the past two years in the far north of Scotland, in Caithness. www.jeart.eu

KAREN FRASER is Executive Manager for Shetland Library, Lerwick.

NIKOLAI GLOBE is a ceramic artist working on the Isle of Harris. High-fired earthenware, porcelain, stoneware and local minerals are his palette, and the terrain of the Hebrides his muse.

RODY GORMAN was born in Dublin, Ireland in 1960 and now lives in the Isle of Skye, Scotland. He has published ten collections of poetry in English, Irish and Scottish Gaelic. His selected poems in Irish and Scottish Gaelic, Chernilo, was published by Coiscéim in 2006.

DEREK GRAY is Artificer of Arts Complex, St Margaret's House, Edinburgh.

CHRISTINE GUNN is Education Officer at Caithness Horizons, Thurso.

GEORGE GUNN was born in Thurso in 1956, where he still lives. A play-wright, poet and journalist he has produced several series for BBC Radio Scotland and Radio 4, and his collections include Black Fish (Scotia Review, 2004), Winter Barley (Chapman, 2005) and The Atlantic Forest (Two Ravens Press, 2008).

THORVALDUR GYLFASON is Professor of Economics at the University of Iceland. He was one of 25 representatives in Iceland's Constitutional Council in session from 1 April to 29 July 2011, elected by the nation and appointed by parliament to revise Iceland's constitution.

JOHN HENDY QC practises predominantly in the field of industrial relations and has appeared in most of the leading cases on industrial action and collective bargaining in the last 30 years. He is Standing Counsel to eight British unions. He is President of the International Centre for Trade Union Rights and Chair of the Institute of Employment Rights. He is a visiting professor at King's College, London and at University College,

London. In 2011 he received a Lifetime Achievement Award from Liberty for his work on workers' and trade union rights and was the Employment Silk of the Year, 2013 (awarded by the Legal 500).

IAIN HUNTER has worked in the defence electro-optics and computer service industries and is currently preparing for retirement. He shares his time between Ayrshire and Sutherland.

JOHN LISTER was formerly Head of Classics at the Edinburgh Academy.

SARAH MASON is proprietor of Mason's Shoes, 80 High St, Dunbar.

MAIRI MORRISON lives in North Uist. She has worked as a secondary school teacher, a researcher and teacher trainer, and now works part-time at Cothrom, the Adult Learning Centre. She is a volunteer and researcher for the museum at Taigh Chearsabagh and sings in the local Gaelic choir.

DAVE MOXHAM is deputy General Secretary of the STUC.

DAVID PROSSER is Head of Art at the Edinburgh Academy.

ANGUS REID is an independent artist. His films include Brotherly Love, The Ring (Winner: Best Central European Documentary Feature 2004) and Primary School Musical!; his books include three collections of poetry, *The Gift, White Medicine* and *The Book of Days* (Caseroom Press 2012) from which the constitution poem is drawn. He lives and works in Edinburgh. www.angusreid.co.uk

LAURA SIMPSON was assistant curator for exhibitions at DJCAD, Dundee.

GRACE VICKERS was Head Teacher at St Thomas of Aquins High School, Edinburgh from 2008–2013, and is now Quality Improvement Manager for Schools and Communities at the City of Edinburgh Council.

DANNY ZINKUS is a council member of Unlock Democracy, the UK's leading campaign for democracy, Rights and Freedoms. He is a qualified accountant and an associate of the Chartered Institute of Management Accountants. He has a career in planning and managing organisations, both private sector and not-for-profit, and has served at board level for both businesses and charities.

Bibliography

POETRY

The Book of Days, Angus Reid, Caseroom Press, 2013

CIVIL RIGHTS

The Rights of Man, Thomas Paine, Dover Publications, 2000
A Vindication of the Rights of Women, Mary Wollstonecraft, Dover
  Publications, 1996
The Spirit Level: why equality is better for everyone, Richard
  Wilkinson and Kate Pickett, Allan Books 2009, Penguin Books,
  2010

HISTORY

Comrade or Brother? A History of the British Labour Movement,
  Mary Davis, Pluto Press, 1993, 2009
Sylvia Pankhurst: A Life in Radical Politics, Mary Davis, Pluto Press,
  1999
Class and Gender in British Labour History, Mary Davis, Merlin
  Press, 2011
The Levellers and the English Revolution, H. N. Brailsford,
  Spokesman books, 1976
The Putney Debates, (*Revolutions Series*) Geoffrey Robertson, Verso,
  2007
The World Turned Upsidedown, Christopher Hill, Penguin, 1991
The Century of Revolution, Christopher Hill, Routledge, 2001
Cromwell and Communism, Eduard Bernstein, Spokesman books, 2001
Contemporary Histories of the English Civil War, Brian Manning (ed)
  Caliban books, 1999
The Scottish Revolution 1637–44, David Stevenson, Birlinn, 2003
Revolution and Counter Revolution 1644–51, David Stevenson,
  Birlinn, 2003

James Connolly, Collected works vols I and II, New Books publications, 1987/8

A Lost Left: 3 studies in Socialism and Nationalism, David Howell, Manchester University Press, 1986

THE 2014 REFERENDUM

A Model Constitution for Scotland: making democracy work, W Elliot Bulmer, Luath Press, 2011

The Battle for Britain: Scotland and the Independence Referendum, David Torrance, Biteback, 2013

Class, Nation and Socialism: The Red Paper on Scotland 2014, Pauline Bryan and Tommy Kane (ed), Glasgow Caledonian University Archives, 2013

Scotland's Future, The Scottish Government, 2013

Scotland's Future: from the Referendum to Independence and a written constitution, The Scottish Government, 2013

If you agree with these principles, and wish the
Scottish Parliament to overcome its reluctance to debate them,
please sign the online petition here:

www.callforaconstitution.co.uk

*if you agree with these principles
please leave a handprint*

Some other books published by **LUATH** PRESS

Blossom: What Scotland Needs to Flourish

Lesley Riddoch
ISBN: 978-1-908373-69-4 PBK £11.99

 Weeding out vital components of Scottish identity from decades of political and social tangle is no mean task, but it's one journalist Lesley Riddoch has undertaken.

Dispensing with the tired, yo-yoing jousts over fiscal commissions, devo something-or-other and EU in-or-out, *Blossom* pinpoints both the buds of growth and the blight that's holding Scotland back. Drawing from its people and history, as well as the experience of the Nordic countries and the author's own passionate and outspoken perspective, this is a plain-speaking but incisive call to restore equality and control to local communities and let Scotland flourish.

Not so much an intervention in the independence debate as a heartfelt manifesto for a better democracy.
THE SCOTSMAN

After Independence: An informed guide to Scotland's possible futures for anyone who is pro or anti independence, unsure or just generally curious

Edited by Gerry Hassan and James Mitchell
ISBN: 978-1-908373-95-3 PBK £12.99

 At the height of the Scottish Independence debate, *After Independence* offers an in-depth and varied exploration of the possibilities for Scotland from both pro- and anti-independence standpoints.

Drawing together over two dozen leading minds on the subject, *After Independence* offers a comprehensive and balanced analysis of Scotland's current and prospective political, economic, social and cultural situation.

Brought together in an inclusive, accessible and informative way, *After Independence* asks and answers a range of questions crucial to the Independence debate and invites its readers to become involved at this crucial moment of Scottish history in the making.

Details of these and other books published by Luath Press can be found at:
www.luath.co.uk

Luath Press Limited

committed to publishing well written books worth reading

LUATH PRESS takes its name from Robert Burns, whose little collie Luath (*Gael.*, swift or nimble) tripped up Jean Armour at a wedding and gave him the chance to speak to the woman who was to be his wife and the abiding love of his life. Burns called one of 'The Twa Dogs' Luath after Cuchullin's hunting dog in Ossian's *Fingal*. Luath Press was established in 1981 in the heart of Burns country, and now resides a few steps up the road from Burns' first lodgings on Edinburgh's Royal Mile.

Luath offers you distinctive writing with a hint of unexpected pleasures.

Most bookshops in the UK, the US, Canada, Australia, New Zealand and parts of Europe either carry our books in stock or can order them for you. To order direct from us, please send a £sterling cheque, postal order, international money order or your credit card details (number, address of cardholder and expiry date) to us at the address below. Please add post and packing as follows: UK – £1.00 per delivery address; overseas surface mail – £2.50 per delivery address; overseas airmail – £3.50 for the first book to each delivery address, plus £1.00 for each additional book by airmail to the same address. If your order is a gift, we will happily enclose your card or message at no extra charge.

Luath Press Limited
543/2 Castlehill
The Royal Mile
Edinburgh EH1 2ND
Scotland
Telephone: 0131 225 4326 (24 hours)
Fax: 0131 225 4324
email: sales@luath.co.uk
Website: www.luath.co.uk